MY TURN

HILLARY CLINTON
TARGETS THE PRESIDENCY

DOUG
HENWOOD

SEVEN STORIES PRESS
NEW YORK · OAKLAND

First published in the United States by OR Books LLC, New York, 2015.

Copyright © 2015 by Doug Henwood

First Seven Stories Press edition May 2016.

Seven Stories Press
140 Watts Street
New York, NY 10013
sevenstories.com

ISBN 978-1-60980-756-6

Library of Congress Control Number: 2016936616

Printed in the United States of America

9 8 7 6 5 4 3 2 1

Cover art reprinted by permission of OR Press.

"My two cents' worth—and I think it is the two cents' worth of everybody who worked for the Clinton Administration health care reform effort of 1993–1994—is that Hillary Rodham Clinton needs to be kept very far away from the White House for the rest of her life. Heading up health-care reform was the only major administrative job she has ever tried to do. And she was a complete flop at it. She had neither the grasp of policy substance, the managerial skills, nor the political smarts to do the job she was then given. And she wasn't smart enough to realize that she was in over her head and had to get out of the Health Care Czar role quickly.... Hillary Rodham Clinton has already flopped as a senior administrative official in the executive branch—the equivalent of an Undersecretary. Perhaps she will make a good senator. But there is no reason to think that she would be anything but an abysmal president."[1]

—Brad DeLong, undersecretary of the Treasury in the first
Clinton administration, 1993–1995, writing in 2003.
At first, DeLong didn't respond to multiple queries about
whether he still believes this. He doesn't.

CONTENTS

INTRODUCTION

To answer Sarah Palin's question (from a 2010 speech), "that hopey, changey stuff" is not working out so well.[2] We avoided depression after the 2008 crash, but the job market remains sick. The headline unemployment rate looks good, but that's because so many people have dropped out of the labor force and aren't counted as jobless. It would take the creation of over eight million new jobs to get back to the share of the population that was employed before the Great Recession hit. It's not seen as eccentric to talk about global capitalism having fallen into structural stagnation—though the rich are doing fine. Incomes are distributed more unequally than they were in 2008, when Obama was elected, and the poverty rate is higher. Obama has, if anything, governed more secretively than Bush. He prosecutes leakers more intensely and kills alleged terrorists that Bush would merely have tortured. The climate crisis gets worse, and the political capacity even to talk about it, much less do anything about it, seems yet unborn. In a move that perfectly captures what Walter

Benn Michaels calls the left wing of neoliberalism, Obama went to Alaska and announced that the federal government would henceforth call Mount McKinley (named after the hard-money imperialist president) by its native name, Denali (something the state has done for 40 years)—and, two days later, allowed Shell to drill more deeply than ever before in the waters off Alaska. Shell changed its mind with the collapse of oil prices, but Obama was happy to let them have their way.

These aren't the complaints Sarah Palin would make, of course. But people who voted for Barack Obama in 2008 were imagining a more peaceful, more egalitarian world, and haven't gotten it.

And who was the front-runner going into the 2016 campaign? Hillary Clinton, who is hardly the first name that comes to mind when one thinks of transformative change.

The case for Hillary boils down to this: she has experience, she's a woman, and it's her turn. Even ardent supporters seem to have a hard time making a substantive political argument in her favor. She has, in the past, been associated with "women's and children's" issues, but she supported her husband's signing the bill that put the end to welfare. "We have to do what we have to do, and I hope our friends understand it," she told their long-time advisor Dick Morris.[3] Morris, who now is a right-wing pundit for the Fox demographic, credits her for backing two of Bill's most important moves to the center after the electoral debacle of 1994—"the balanced budget and welfare reform."[4]

As wacky as it sometimes appears on the surface, American politics has an amazing stability and continuity about it. According to Gallup, just 29% of Americans have either "a great deal" or "quite a lot" of confidence in the institution of the presidency, and only 7% do in Congress. Nor do they have much faith in other institutions, like banks, the health care system, the media, big business, or organized labor.[5] But the leading candidate for the presidency is one of the original architects of the New Democrat strategy back in the 1980s. That itself was a consolidation of the Reagan revolution—an acknowledgment that movement conservatism had come to set the terms of American political discourse.

Obama himself said as much during the 2008 campaign, when he declared that "Ronald Reagan changed the trajectory of America in a way that, you know, Richard Nixon did not and in a way that Bill Clinton did not. He put us on a fundamentally different path because the country was ready for it. I think they felt like, you know, with all the excesses of the 60s and the 70s, and government had grown and grown, but there wasn't much sense of accountability in terms of how it was operating."[6] The "excesses of the 60s and 70s" included things like feminism, gay liberation, the antiwar movement, wildcat strikes, and a militant antiracist uprising. I find those all to be good things, but I know that some people disagree.

Later in those comments, in an interview with a Reno TV station, Obama said that "the Republicans were the party of ideas for a pretty long chunk of time there over the last 10, 15 years, in the sense that they were challenging conventional wisdom. Now, you've heard it all before." Though he didn't claim the status—"I don't want to present myself as some sort of singular figure"—he did suggest that the times were changing, and he was the agent of that change.

But they didn't and he wasn't. Coming into office with something like a mandate to reverse the miserable policies of the Bush era, Obama never tried to make a sharp political break with the past, as Reagan did from the moment of his first inaugural address. Reagan dismissed the postwar Keynesian consensus—the idea that government had a responsibility to soften the sharpest edges of capitalism by fighting recession and providing some sort of basic safety net—as the tired policies of the past. Appropriating some of the spirit and language of the left about revolution and the promise of a shiny future, Reagan unleashed what he liked to call the magic of the marketplace—cutting taxes for the rich, eliminating regulations, squeezing social spending, and celebrating the accumulation of money.

While it's easy to dismiss Reagan's appeal to freedom as propaganda for the corporate class and a blueprint for the upward redistribution of income—because that's exactly what it was from a ruling-class POV—it's also unfair to Reagan. He really believed in the liberating power of unfettered markets. He emerged from movement conservatism, a coherent political philosophy. In that sense, Obama was right about Reagan.

From the point of view of the American elite, the 1970s were a miserable decade. Corporate profits were depressed, inflation was rising, financial markets were sputtering, the United States had lost the Vietnam War, and the working class was in a state of rebellion. CEOs felt besieged; in a 1975 survey of *Harvard Business Review* subscribers, almost three-quarters saw some form of socialism prevailing by 1985.[7]

By the end of the 1970s, feeding off popular discontent, elites led a rightward turn in our politics. Paul Volcker, appointed to the chairmanship of the Federal Reserve by Jimmy Carter in 1979, engineered a deep recession. The following year, Ronald Reagan was elected president, proclaiming a new order in which government was the problem that had to be kicked out of the way to let the marketplace work its magic. He fired striking air traffic controllers, setting the precedent for open warfare on unions, and remade fiscal policy into a scheme for making the rich richer at the expense of everyone else. Wages stagnated, and employment became considerably less secure. Workers who in the 1970s were slacking off on the job or going out on strike would no longer dream of misbehaving. The "cure" worked. A strange and unequal boom took hold that lasted into the early 1990s. After the caretaker George H.W. Bush administration evaporated, Bill Clinton took over, and with a few minor adjustments, kept the boom going for another decade. Profits zoomed, as did financial markets; 1985 (and 1995) turned out to be rather different from what the executive class had feared in 1975.

But a contradiction lay beneath it all: a system dependent on high levels of mass consumption for both economic dynamism and political legitimacy has a problem when mass purchasing power is squeezed. For a few decades, consumers borrowed to make up for what their paychecks were lacking, but that model broke down with the crisis of 2008. Today, we desperately need a new model of political economy—one that features a more equal distribution of income, investment in our rotting social and physical infrastructure, and a more cooperative ethic. When one meditates on that constellation, Hillary Clinton does not play a promising role.

In what follows, I'm going to spend some time on the early phase of Hillary's life and career. I think that these stories are an important antidote to liberals' fantasies about her as some sort of great progressive. I'm going to spend less time on analyzing her current policy proposals because, based on her record, there are few reasons for receiving them with anything but profound skepticism.

Although this is a polemic directed at a prominent figure, I also want to make clear from the first that Hillary is not The Problem. (I should also say, because most truths are not self-evident, that all the misogynist attacks on her are grotesque.) By all orthodox measures she is a highly intelligent and informed senior member of the political class. That is the problem. Hillary is a symptom of a deep sickness in the American political system, produced by the structural features designed to limit popular power that James Madison first mused about in *The Federalist Papers* and that the authors of the Constitution inscribed in our basic law. Those inhibiting Constitutional features include the division of power among the branches, judicial review, and the deeply undemocratic structure of the Senate, all supplemented with a variety of schemes over the decades to limit the franchise. Add to that the quasi-official status of a two-party Congress, the ability of the rich to buy legislation and legislators, and the gatekeeping role of the media and you have a system that offers voters little more than the choice of which branch of the elite is going to screw them. And this doesn't even get to the increase in presidential powers over the last few decades, a structural problem that is far larger than the inhabitant of the office.[8]

While it's sometimes fashionable to complain that our democracy has been taken from us, things have always been pretty much this way. It's this system that produces the likes of Hillary (and Jeb, and Marco, and all the rest, with oddballs like Donald occasionally crashing the party). And it's why this book doesn't end with a call to arms for an opposing candidate, since anyone likely to be elected is going to be from the same mold. Hillary is undeniably good at politics, even though she lacks her husband's charm. But she is basically a standard-issue mainstream—or, as we used to say in bolder times, bourgeois—politician. This book is meant to refute all the extravagant claims from her supporters that she is more than that. And explain why her aura of inevitability going into this campaign, substantially diminished by the fall of 2015, was her major asset.

It may seem odd, in introducing a book devoted to a presidential candidate, to demean the political importance of presidential elections, but that's what I'm about to do. That's not to say the office isn't important. Of course it is. Although the president's room for maneuver is constrained by other branches and levels of government, not to mention ruling class power, it is still the most important political position in the world. The U.S. president is essentially the chief executive of the global elite. The international lines of command aren't as clear as they once were; it's hilarious to hear presidential candidates compete over who'd be the toughest on China, a country to which our Treasury owes $1.2 trillion.[9] But there's no more powerful single office anywhere in the world, and elites have a lock on it.

Anyone who wants seriously better politics in this country has to start from the bottom and work their way up. So while I may have some good things to say about Bernie Sanders and his campaign, magical interventions from the top won't change much. If, by some freakish accident, Sanders ever got elected, the established order would crush him. We'll never find salvation, or even decency, from above.

A note on usage: most of the time I refer to Hillary Rodham Clinton by her first name alone. Aside from its brevity, it distinguishes her from her husband, whom I mostly call Bill. It is also how she has been branding herself since her first run for the Senate—as the quirky but often sharp Dick Morris, who's known her since 1978, put it, "symbolically independent of Bill and the tarnished Clinton name."[10]

1 FROM PARK RIDGE TO LITTLE ROCK

Hillary Rodham spent her early years in Park Ridge, Illinois, a dry (as in drink-free), WASPy suburb of Chicago. In her childrearing book, *It Takes a Village*, she says she "grew up in a family that looked like it was straight out of the 1950s television sitcom *Father Knows Best*. Hugh Ellsworth Rodham, my father, was a self-sufficient, tough-minded small-businessman who ran a plant that screen-printed and sold drapery fabrics."[11] This description of her father seems generous about a man who, by Gail Sheehy's rendition, was emotionally abusive and impossible to please. She describes a supportive village surrounding her in childhood: "Grandparents, aunts, uncles, and cousins all pitched in if illness or some other misfortune strained the family."[12] As Carl Bernstein notes in his biography of Hillary, "She does not mention such misfortunes as her father cutting his brother down from a noose."[13]

Hillary has a long history of being economical with the truth—which is why Bernstein says of her voluminous but

minimally informative memoir *Living History* that its "princi-
pal value…is as insight into how Hillary sees herself and wants
the story of her life to be told. It is often at variance with my
reporting, other books, and with newspapers and periodicals
as well."[14]

One can forgive Hillary's reticence about sharing the un-
pleasantries of her childhood. But her early environment resem-
bled the world of Thomas Hobbes more than that of 1950s TV. As
Gail Sheehy reported, Hugh Rodham was a gruff, "authoritarian
drillmaster," a political reactionary who demanded austerity, discipline, and self-reliance. Displays of emotion were regarded as
signs of weakness.[15] Her mother, Dorothy Howell, had a rough
childhood. Born to a 15-year-old mother, Dorothy had parents
who split up when she was eight and disappeared from her life.
She was left in the care of what Sheehy describes as a "demeaning"
grandmother who then fobbed her off on strangers who worked
her for room and board.[16] Hillary told a college classmate that
her parents' fights were so distressing that she felt as if she was
losing the top of her head.[17] It was an atmosphere that demanded
toughness and self-reliance.

Young Hillary picked up the conservatism of her father and
her surroundings. In junior high, she fell under the influence of
a history teacher, Paul Carlson, a follower of the frothing anti-
communist senator Joe McCarthy. As Carlson told Sheehy, the

young Hillary was "a hawk."[18] A few years later, though, she found another guru, one she'd stick with for years—a young new pastor at the First Methodist Church of Park Ridge named Don Jones. (Hillary has always been very much a Methodist.) Jones was a dashing intellectual who helped open Hillary's mind. He got the church youth reading D.H. Lawrence and e.e. cummings, listening to Bob Dylan, and talking about Picasso. He took his flock to the South Side of Chicago to meet some black youth.[19] But despite this new affiliation, she hadn't given up on the reactionary Carlson—she joined his discussion club to get a taste of his roster of hard-right speakers.[20] In April 1962, Jones took her to hear Martin Luther King Jr. speak in Chicago, and then meet him backstage. She was moved, but not enough to stop her from campaigning for Barry Goldwater—a man whose candidacy was the overture to the right's long rise in American politics—in 1964.[21]

Though it's sometimes occluded by rhetoric and gestures, like the austere Protestantism, that conservative political streak never went away. Hillary fans dismiss her Goldwater fandom as a youthful indiscretion, but she professed a continuing allegiance in a 1996 interview: "I feel like my political beliefs are rooted in the conservatism that I was raised with. I don't recognize this new brand of Republicanism that is afoot now, which I consider to be very reactionary, not conservative in many respects. I am very proud that I was a Goldwater girl."[22] Her distinction between "reactionary" and "conservative" is hard to parse; Goldwater voted against the 1964 Civil Rights Act, wanted to privatize Social Security, and once suggested that we "lob one into the men's room at the Kremlin."

Then she was off to Wellesley. In Sheehy's words (quoting from letters to a high school friend), "Her first order of business was to choose an identity. That's right, choose. Over Christmas vacation in her sophomore year, by her own count, she went through no fewer than 'three-and-a-half metamorphoses.' Hillary Rodham was fully conscious of selecting her preferred personality from a 'smorgasbord' spread before her: 'educational and social reformer, alienated academic, involved pseudohippie,' political leader, or 'compassionate misanthrope.'"[23]

A few years into college, she began feeling seriously alienated from "the entire unreality of middle-class America." But she was not about to become a student revolutionary: identifying herself as an "agnostic intellectual liberal [and] emotional conservative," she would "work toward change by keeping her peers in line as they protested," as Sheehy put it.[24] Or, in the words of the then-president of Wellesley, she was all about "effecting change… from within rather than outside the system."[25]

Hillary wrote her undergraduate thesis on the founder of community organizing, Saul Alinsky. (Curiously, Barack Obama has a reputed history as a community organizer in the Alinsky tradition. Chicago activists can't recall much of significance that he did, but it has yielded him some largely unearned cred on the left and thoroughly unearned antipathy on the right.) Her advisor, Alan Schechter, told Bill Clinton's biographer David Maraniss that she "started out thinking community action programs would make a big difference," but came around to thinking that they were "too idealistic and simplistic; that they might make a marginal but not a lasting difference," because they needed outside money and help.[26] Hillary has never been one for organization from below.

There's a foretaste of the future Hillary in this characterization of Alinsky's thinking from her thesis: "Welfare programs since the New Deal have neither redeveloped poverty areas nor even catalyzed the poor into helping themselves. A cycle of dependency has been created which ensnares its victims into resignation and apathy."[27] While there's an element of truth to this, Alinsky's remedy was for poor people to claim political power on their own behalf (leaving aside the question of whether his organizing techniques could accomplish that). Hillary, though, would support welfare "reform" in the 1990s, throwing single mothers onto the mercies of the low-wage job market. Though her support for welfare reform was partly an act of political cynicism—she thought it would get her husband votes—there was plenty of the moral astringency of the old English workhouse about it too.

During Hillary's senior year, a movement arose to have a student speaker at graduation, and Hillary emerged as the consensus candidate for the job. Her remarks, though enthusiastically received, meander all over the page when read as a text 45 years later. What stands out, though, is this remarkable passage:

> We are, all of us, exploring a world that none of us even understands and attempting to create within that uncertainty. But there are some things we feel, feelings that our prevailing, acquisitive, and competitive corporate life, including tragically the universities, is not the way of life for us. We're searching for more immediate, ecstatic, and penetrating modes of living.[28]

That is not the Hillary we know today. But, as odd as it sounds, years later, her husband would say this to the National Association of Realtors in 1993: "I used to save a little quote by Carl Sandburg.... Sandburg said, a tough will counts. So does desire. So does a rich, soft wanting.... I see that and I think you do too."[29] Who knew that under all that duplicity and ambition, they're just a pair of Romantics?

The practical Hillary nonetheless overruled the ecstatic and penetrating Hillary—she rejected an organizing job offered by Alinsky to go to law school. He said, "Well, that's no way to change anything." She responded: "Well, I see a different way from you. And I think there is a real opportunity."[30] And it was on to the Yale Law School.

While it's widely known that Hillary and Bill met when they were students at Yale, it's less known that their first date essentially involved crossing a picket line. Bill suggested they go to a Rothko exhibit at the university's art gallery, but it was closed because of a campus-wide strike by unionized employees. Bill convinced a guard to let them in, after he cleared away the garbage blocking the entrance.[31] Hillary was impressed—not for the first time—by his powers of persuasion. Soon after, Bill "'locked in on' her," as Maraniss put it.[32] Hillary found him "complex," with "lots of layers."[33]

By Yale Law standards, one friend recalled to Maraniss, Hillary was a conservative—though she opposed the Vietnam War and dressed like a hippie, she still believed in the fundamental institutions of American life.[34] She had no patience for the utopianism of the time.

The year after she graduated from law school in 1972, she wrote a paper for the *Harvard Educational Review* on the legal rights of children. She'd gotten interested in the topic after hearing Marian Wright Edelman—the first black woman admitted to the Mississippi bar—lecture at Yale.[35] After the lecture, she approached Edelman, asking to work with her at her D.C.-based public interest law firm, where Hillary then spent the summer of 1970 working on issues related to the conditions of migrant farm laborers and their families.

Although the right would later denounce her article as a radical anti-family screed, it was anything but. Hillary concluded that the state had to intervene in the case of actual harm to children, but the governing standard had to be strict. Offensive but not objective "medically diagnosable harm" should not trigger intervention.[36] It was the first in a series of legal articles on children and families, an early instance of what she would later describe as a life-long interest in such issues. Her relationship to child welfare—and to Marian Wright Edelman—would change dramatically when Bill signed the welfare reform bill 20 years later, and a different view of poor children (and their mothers) became more expedient.[37] Edelman called it a "moment of shame," and her husband, Peter Edelman, resigned from the Clinton administration with an open letter of protest.[38]

Soon after his graduation, Bill returned to Arkansas—first for a stint as a law professor, and then to run for Congress. John Doar, who was putting together the legal team for the Nixon impeachment case, offered Bill a job, but Bill suggested that he instead hire Hillary, who was by then working at Edelman's Children's Defense Fund. Bill was taking the long view. Maraniss cites a conversation Bill had with Arkansas politician

David Pryor: "[A]ccording to Pryor, Clinton put the question in terms of his friend Rodham and his relationship with her. 'He talked to me about Hillary going to work for the Watergate committee,' Pryor recalled. 'He asked, "Is that a good idea?" It was a career consideration. He knew that his career would be in politics and the question was whether Hillary's connection with the Watergate committee might have political ramifications.'"[39]

Hillary took the job. She became friends with Bernard Nussbaum, one of Doar's top assistants, who'd later become Bill's White House Counsel. She told him—and anyone else who'd listen—that Bill was destined to be president someday. Nussbaum thought that was ridiculous. Hillary exploded at him: "You asshole.... He is going to be president of the United States."[40] (Hillary apparently often swears like a longshoreman, one of the more endearing things about her.) But expectations were also high for Hillary. A couple of years earlier, when she was working on the McGovern campaign, her colleagues thought she had a great political career ahead of her.[41] Bill himself thought she could be a senator or governor someday.[42]

So what to do after the impeachment committee dissolved? She could go back to the Children's Defense Fund. She could go to Washington and work at a law firm, get a feel for politics—a route complicated by her having failed the D.C. bar exam (something she kept secret for 30 years).[43] Or she could relocate to Arkansas, where she'd visited a few times, to be with Bill.[44] Moving to the sticks made her nervous, but she headed there anyway, joining Bill while his 1974 Congressional campaign was underway. Bill lost, but he'd made a name for himself, almost beating an incumbent against long odds.

He immediately began thinking of the next race. His eye was on the governorship, but he calculated that attorney general might be a more achievable first step. Hillary was teaching law and running a legal aid clinic. They spent lots of time together, but marriage was still an open question. She had political ambitions, and worried that she'd be seen as a bad feminist if she acquired family obligations. She took a trip east and asked her friends about the wisdom of marrying Bill. When she got back to Arkansas, Bill greeted her with the news of a house he'd just bought and a marriage proposal. She accepted.[45]

During the attorney general campaign, Bill alienated the state's unions by refusing to support the repeal of Arkansas' right-to-work law. It was the first in a long line of gestures with which he aimed to distance himself from traditional liberal politics.[46] He won this election handily—though everyone was aware that the office was just a stepping stone.

The young couple moved from the relatively bohemian Fayetteville to the more formal Little Rock. Hillary went from the legal clinic to the Rose Law Firm, which represented the moneyed interests of Arkansas. It did not hurt her prospects at the firm that her husband was the state's chief legal officer, albeit one not long for the job. Less than a year after the election, Bill's chief of staff called in a neophyte political consultant from New York, Dick Morris, to evaluate his next step—governor or senator? Morris counseled a run for governor. It was the beginning of a 20-year association, interrupted by occasional storms, between the wily psephologist and the two Clintons.

While Hillary was at Rose, her allegiances began to shift. The community organizing group ACORN, then based in Arkansas and very much in the Alinsky tradition, got a ballot measure passed that would lower electricity rates for residential users in Little Rock and raise them for commercial users. Business, of course, was not pleased, and filed a legal challenge, with Rose representing them. Wade Rathke, the founder of ACORN who'd been a friend of Hillary's, was shocked to see her arguing the business case in court. And not only did she argue the case—she helped, too, to craft the legal strategy, which was that the new rate schedule amounted to an unconstitutional "taking of property." This is now a common right-wing argument against regulation. Hillary was one of its early architects.

A few years later, she handled a case for Rose on behalf of Coca-Cola. Coke had been sued by a worker who claimed that he was disabled and had been improperly denied retirement benefits. Taking this assignment stood in stark contrast with Hillary's attitude earlier in the decade, when she'd criticized the hotshot D.C. lawyer Joseph Califano for defending Coke's treatment of migrant farm workers in characteristically pithy terms: "You sold out, you motherfucker, you sold out."[47] Hillary had evidently come a long way from defending children, or her summer internship during law school at a radical law firm in Oakland where two of the partners were Communists.[48]

Bill won the 1978 election and embraced as one of his signature programs the improvement of Arkansas' miserable road system. He chose to finance it by raising car license fees—which proved enormously unpopular, and was a major reason he lost his bid for re-election two years later. (Arkansas governors served only two-year terms in those days.) With the help of Dick Morris, Bill began plotting his comeback almost as soon as the ballots were counted. Morris' polling discovered that the people of Arkansas generally liked Bill, but saw him as someone who'd been led astray by the countercultural types who populated Yale and Oxford (where Bill was a Rhodes scholar after graduating from college). Morris advised him to offer a public mea culpa on the car tax, which he did. And Hillary, who'd been sticking with the surname Rodham like the 1970s feminist she saw herself as, now took the Clinton name.[49] Bill went on to recapture the governorship. As a result of this experience, he, Hillary, and Morris together decided that the best way to conduct politics was through permanent campaigning.[50] Policy and polling would be inseparable.

This model of governing depended on finding reliable enemies who could be relentlessly attacked. Bill, with advice from Morris and close support from Hillary, chose the teachers' union. A court had ruled the Arkansas education finance system unconstitutional. It was certainly woefully unequal, with teachers in some districts paid so poorly that they qualified for Food Stamps.[51] Raising taxes was a political challenge, however, so Clinton proposed balancing a one point increase in the sales tax with a competency test for teachers, something that the teachers' union vigorously opposed. Morris had discovered that the Arkansas public was not at all fond of the union. Tying the test to the tax increase allowed Clinton to present himself as doing it all for the kids, and not a special interest group. Morris celebrated the maneuver as a politically crafty break from the ways of the Old Democrat left.

As Carl Bernstein put it in his biography of Hillary, the teachers' union "was not exactly the antichrist, and in fact had done some pretty good things in a state where the legislature had typically accorded more attention to protecting the rights of poultry farmers to saturate half of Arkansas' topsoil with chicken feces than providing its children with a decent education."[52] But setting up the union as the enemy paid rich political dividends. Clinton got the tax increase and the competency test. These measures did not, however, lead to any improvement in Arkansas' educational performance.[53] A review of the reform efforts by the Winthrop Rockefeller Foundation found "a serious, large demoralization of the teaching force. They feel constrained by what they perceive to be a stranglehold of mandates, needless paperwork and limited encouragement."[54] The problems of Arkansas' educational system were so deeply structural, rooted in the state's poverty and backwardness, that tackling them required a wholesale overhaul of the state's entire political economy. The Clintons weren't about to take that on.

Instead, they were laying the groundwork for the creation of what would eventually hit the national stage as the New Democrat movement, something that took institutional form in the Democratic Leadership Council that was set up in 1985. Support for teacher testing and the right-to-work law were effective ways to show the Clintons' distance from organized labor. Bill went light on environmental enforcement and spread around tax breaks in the name of "economic development." Tyson Foods, the major producer of the chicken shit referred to by Bernstein, got

$8 million in tax breaks between 1988 and 1990, at a time when the company's budget was twice that of the entire state.[55] Hillary was at Bill's side throughout all of this and was a close collaborator in the education reform operation. She co-wrote Bill's 1991 keynote speech at the DLC's national convention, which turned out to be a major hit. It was an early declaration of New Democrat principles—the promotion of "personal responsibility" as the solution to social problems, the evocation of the beauties of free trade and fiscal discipline, the excoriation of "government monopoly," the treatment of "citizens like...customers," movement beyond the presumably obsolete categories of left and right, and promises of enhanced "opportunity" for all. Those promises of opportunity would recur throughout his presidency, but were never backed up with much in the way of budget allocations.[56]

But Hillary wasn't just doing political work for the Clinton enterprise; she was also busy defending the leading lights of Arkansas Inc. at Rose and serving on various corporate boards—most notoriously, the viciously anti-union Wal-Mart. (In her defense, she did encourage the firm to begin a recycling program.)[57] In her six years on the Wal-Mart board, from 1986 to 1992, Hillary did not utter a single word of opposition to the company's hostility to unions, nor is there any evidence that she challenged the company's notorious discrimination against women in pay and promotion. On the contrary, at a 1990 stockholders' meeting she expressed her pride in the company, and founder Sam Walton used her presence on the board to deflect criticism of the company's sexist practices.[58] When asked in 2008 by ABC News about Wal-Mart's hardline anti-labor stance, she could only respond by retreating into generality, saying that unions "have been essential to our nation's success."[59]

Connections between Rose and the state of Arkansas would later cause the Clintons no end of problems, and not just for the circus that came to be known as Whitewater. The state did all kinds of business with Rose, from routine bond issues to more complex litigation.[60] Having the state do business with a law firm that employed the governor's wife seemed a little smelly to many. But, no matter—the Clintons would soon be leaving town. Ambitions as expansive as theirs couldn't be satisfied in the Ozarks.

2 FIRST LADY

The Clintons had outgrown Arkansas. Bill contemplated running for president in 1988. He decided against it, in part because he was terrified that one or more of a wide variety of paramours would come forward with their stories.[61] But he eventually found his nerve and plunged into the 1992 campaign. An internal campaign memo from March of that year, reported by Jeff Gerth and Don Von Natta in their book on Hillary, listed more than 75 potential problems for the candidacy. Among them were, of course, Bill's many affairs, but about two-thirds of the sore spots involved both Bill and Hillary, or Hillary alone. Eighteen of the problems were related to Hillary and her work at Rose.[62]

Despite these difficulties, the Clintons ran a successful campaign. Ross Perot divided the anti–George H.W. Bush vote and Bill won the election with 43% of the vote. It was the next stage of what they'd years earlier called The Journey—their joint venture to change the world. As Gail Sheehy put it: "Eight years of Bill, eight years of Hill. That was the dream. It was Hillary's private slogan, shared with one of her closest intimates, Linda Blood-worth-Thomason. Early in his 1992 presidential campaign, I asked then Governor Clinton if he was concerned about being upstaged by his wife. He was unfazed: 'I've always liked strong women. It doesn't bother me for people to see her and get excited and say she could be president, too.' 'So, after eight years of Bill Clinton?' I teased. 'Eight years of Hillary Clinton,' he said. 'Why not?'"

The inauguration would set the tone for the presidency. Despite their rhetorical efforts to declare an end to the greed and materialism of the 1980s, the event was a model of excess that cost $25 million.[63] The greed and materialism of the 1990s were upon us.

The presidential couple settled into what seemed at first like a co-presidency, with Hillary exercising an influence that no previous First Lady ever had. This caused trouble right from the start. Always suspicious of the media, she shut off reporters' access to the West Wing of the White House. The move ended up alienating the press to no good effect.

More substantively, Hillary was given responsibility for running the health care reform agenda. It was very much a New Democrat scheme. Rejecting a Canadian-style single-payer system, Hillary came up with an impossibly complex arrangement called "managed competition." Employers would be encouraged to provide health care to their workers, individuals would be assembled into cooperatives with some bargaining power, and competition among providers would keep costs down. But the plan was hatched in total secrecy, with no attempt to cultivate support in Congress or among the public for what would be a massive piece of legislation—and one of which the medical-industrial complex was not at all fond. (The industry's hostility was somewhat mysterious; they feared price controls and bureaucratic meddling in their freedom to do business, but it's not as if Hillary or Bill were out to expropriate them.) At a meeting with Democratic leaders in April 1993, Senator Bill Bradley suggested that Hillary might need to compromise to get a bill passed. She would have none of it: the White House would "demonize" any legislators who stood in her way. Bradley was stunned. Years later, he told Bernstein that "[t]hat was it for me in terms of Hillary Clinton. You don't tell members of the Senate you are going to demonize them. It was obviously so basic to who she is. The arrogance.... The disdain."[64] (You have to love Bradley's assumption that senators should be deferred to.) Health care reform was a miserable failure. It never attracted popular support and went nowhere in Congress. Most of the blame for the failure fell, justifiably, on Hillary.

In an attempt to move on, Hillary now reinvented herself as an "advocate." As she wrote in *Living History*, "I began to focus on discrete domestic projects that were more achievable than massive undertakings such as health care reform. On my agenda now were children's health issues, breast cancer prevention, and protecting funding for public television, legal services and the arts."[65] She campaigned for changes in adoption laws and for a bill to guarantee that newborns and their mothers wouldn't be kicked out of the hospital sooner than 48 hours after the birth.[66] It was all very high-minded, and good for her image, but of limited impact.

She did, however, support one of the most controversial moves of the Clinton years: welfare reform. In *Living History*, she describes it as a "plan that would motivate and equip women to obtain a better life for themselves and their children." She wrote that she'd hoped that welfare reform would have been "the beginning, not the end, of our concern for the poor."[67] This statement is rich in its disingenuousness. The whole point of welfare reform was disciplining the poor, not helping them. Hillary is no naïf and must have recognized that as the political consensus. Still, she bragged that "[b]y the time Bill and I left the White House, welfare rolls had dropped 60 percent from 14.1 million to 5.8 million, and millions of parents had gone to work." Of course, that was during the strongest economic expansion of the last several decades—gains that were undone in the recessions and weak expansions that would follow. Later, as senator, she supported George W. Bush's proposal to expand the work requirement for recipients of the surviving welfare program, Temporary Assistance for Needy Families (TANF)—one of the few Democrats to do so. Advocates for the poor were shocked, showing signs that they were poorly informed about her political history.[68]

A 2014 analysis by the Center on Budget and Policy Priorities found the following about the new welfare regime, Temporary Assistance for Needy Families: fewer families were drawing benefits despite increased need; the value of those benefits have eroded to the point where beneficiaries can't meet their basic needs; it does far less to reduce poverty than its predecessor, Aid to Families with Dependent Children, which welfare reform abolished; and almost all of the early employment gains for single mothers have been reversed.[69]

Living History was written with the help of three ghostwriters, who were thanked in the acknowledgments. The ghostwriter of her earlier book, *It Takes a Village*, wasn't mentioned at all, and Hillary even claimed that she'd written it all herself. When *Village* was announced, the *New York Times* reported that "The book will actually be written by Barbara Feinman, a journalism professor at Georgetown University in Washington. Ms. Feinman will conduct a series of interviews with Mrs. Clinton, who will help edit the resulting text." Feinman even suggested the title, citing an African proverb of dubious provenance. In a 2002 article for a writer's journal, Feinman—then using her married name, Barbara

Feinman Todd—said the book was jointly produced with its editor, exchanging drafts "round-robin style." Several years after the book was published, she told a Washington magazine that Hillary was responsible for Simon & Schuster's delay in paying Todd the final installment of her $120,000 fee. She quoted the publisher as saying, "It's the White House that doesn't want you paid." The non-acknowledgment and withheld installment were widely reported at the time, and an embarrassed Simon & Schuster finally wrote the check.[70]

No survey of Hillary's time as First Lady would be complete without a review of the scandals—and not just Bill's dalliances. The most famous was Whitewater, a word it pains me to type. As Vincent Foster, Hillary's good friend and fellow partner at Rose who came with her to Washington, said in a handwritten note discovered after his suicide, it was "a can of worms you shouldn't open."[71] It's not much fun re-opening it either.

Democrats love to say that there was nothing to Whitewater. While it is certainly true that it was not what Republicans made of it during the impeachment days, neither was it nothing. A sleazy but well-connected pal of the Clintons, Jim McDougal, came to them in 1980 with a proposal to invest in a piece of undeveloped riverfront land in the Ozarks that he hoped to turn into vacation houses. They took up the offer—but paid almost no attention afterward.[72] Had they done so, they might have found that the scheme was not working out. A few years after the land purchase, McDougal bought himself a savings and loan (S&L) that he grandly renamed Madison Guaranty, which he used to fund his real estate ventures, Whitewater among them.[73] Speculators operating on borrowed money are always dangerous—doubly so when they've got their own bank to draw on. And Madison Guaranty, like hundreds of other S&Ls in the early 1980s, was bleeding money. By 1985, a desperate McDougal hired Rose to handle its legal affairs. That was malodorous in itself, since Madison was regulated by the state, and a Rose partner was the governor's wife. But the Clintons were also investors in McDougal's schemes.

The details of the Whitewater scheme are of far less interest than the way Hillary handled it: with lies, half-truths, and secrecy. She initially claimed during the 1992 campaign that she hadn't represented clients before state regulators, which was patently untrue. She then revised that initial position, saying that she'd "tried to avoid such involvement and cannot recall any instance other than the Madison Guaranty matter in which I had any involvement, and my involvement there was minimal." (Madison wasn't the only instance where she had an "involvement." Another was the Southern Development Bancorporation, which paid Rose over $100,000 in fees and received $300,000 in state investments.)[74] On the *Diane Rehm Show*, Hillary said that she'd provided the *New York Times*, which broke the Whitewater story, with "every document we had" about the case. This, too, was completely untrue.[75]

Hillary initially claimed that the Rose billing records for the Madison case, which were under multiple subpoenas, had disappeared. But they suddenly reappeared, discovered by a longtime personal assistant in a room in the residential quarters of the White House. When asked about this mysterious reappearance, Hillary responded, "I, like everyone else, would like to know the answer about how those documents showed up after all these years."[76] The records showed that rather than having a trivial role in representing Madison, she'd actually billed for 60 hours of work.[77]

A prominent legal journalist of my acquaintance, a loyal Hillaryite, explained the fate of the billing documents this way: "They were lost, Doug, and then they were found." There are many dimensions to the Clinton magic.

3 SENATOR

This is a short chapter; there's not a great deal to say about Hillary's Senate career. Aside from her enthusiastic vote for the Iraq War, it's hard to think of her as much more than a seat warmer. In the language of the Senate, she was seen as a workhorse, not a showhorse. There's certainly not much to show for all the work.

At first, Hillary's candidacy for the Senate was seen as a long shot. She set her sights on the New York seat of Daniel "Pat" Moynihan, who was retiring. Whatever his many political problems—like being a pivotal figure in the transformation of the understanding of poverty from a problem endemic to the U.S. economy to cultural pathologies endemic among the poor themselves—Moynihan was nonetheless a substantial figure. Hillary, in contrast, was widely seen as a carpetbagger who knew little of New York and had shown scant interest in it before one if its Senate seats became available. And she could not shake the bad karma from her role at the White House.

She entered the election while she was still First Lady. This required the Clintons to buy a house in Westchester, so she could have a nominal New York residence, which they did two months after she announced, in July 1999, that she was contemplating a run. The location of the announcement was Moynihan's farm, which was supposed to signal his approval. In fact, he'd had troubles with both Clintons dating from the days of health care reform, when the administration, perceiving disloyalty, sprayed him with some hostile leaks. As Carl Bernstein wrote, Moynihan "would make life difficult for the Clintons for years." But he appeared to be mostly over it by 1999.[78]

Although Hillary portrayed herself in *Living History* as at first reluctant to run, only finally deciding to do so on the basis of popular acclamation, Gerth and Van Natta portray her as anything but halting. Her ambition was always intense, certainly no less intense than her husband's. She wanted to be known for her own accomplishments and not as "former First lady" and "derivative spouse."[79]

To counter the carpetbagger problem, Hillary went on a "listening tour" of New York, visiting all of the state's 62 counties, the earliest of her conspicuous exercises in tapping into the *vox populi*. Though there were gaffes, like donning a New York Yankees hat and pretending to be a longtime fan when she wasn't, for which she was widely ridiculed, the tour turned out to be a success, convincing locals that she was like them. All of this was undertaken before she officially announced her candidacy in February 2000. On her campaign merchandise she was simply "Hillary," the first time she'd branded herself without one or two other names.

Her first Republican opponent was New York City mayor Rudy Giuliani, a mean-spirited Republican hardliner. That didn't stop her from trying to take positions to his right. In an interview with the *New York Times*, the first in-depth one of the campaign, "[s]he went out of her way to note her support for the death penalty, welfare restrictions and a balanced budget," as the paper's account put it.[80]

When a diagnosis of prostate cancer forced Giuliani out of the race (which came at the same time he left his wife for another woman, enough to ruin a candidacy on its own), he was replaced by a much weaker candidate, Long Island Congressman Rick Lazio. Hillary beat him comfortably, by 13 points. She would have no trouble getting re-elected in 2006.

Surprisingly, or maybe not, one of her first tasks on arriving in the Senate was making friends with Republicans. In his book, *Clinton, Inc.*, Daniel Halper, a smart, non-frothing conservative, writes:

> Thus what Hillary Clinton pulled off with her Republican Senate colleagues was nothing short of masterful.

I spoke to many, if not all, of Senator Clinton's biggest opponents within the Republican Party during her time as First Lady. On or off the record, no matter how much they were coaxed, not one of them would say a negative thing about Hillary Clinton as a person—other than observing that her Democratic allies sometimes didn't like her.[81]

She buddied up to John McCain, and attended prayer breakfasts with right-wingers like the atrocious Sam Brownback of Kansas (who once described her as "a beautiful child of the living God").[82] She befriended Republicans who'd served as floor managers of her husband's impeachment. Even Newt Gingrich had good things to say about her.[83]

She didn't attend just any prayer breakfasts—she buddied up to the Fellowship, aka the Family, a secretive fundamentalist organization based in Arlington that has long been a gathering place for the political and corporate elite to pray and network. She had been involved with the organization as First Lady and then graduated to its Senatorial branch. Though there are Democrats in the group, it is laced with right-wingers, and as Kathryn Joyce and Jeff Sharlet reported, has a long history of supporting bloody dictators in the name of free enterprise. Its mission has traditionally been to harness a love of Jesus to the running of the world for profit. While there's no doubt a large dose of political expediency in Hillary's association with people that many of her liberal supporters would find appalling, it's also a sign of her residual deep hawkishness and religiosity. As Joyce and Sharlet write, she supported government funding for religiously provided social services before George W. Bush ever did.[84] Her opposition to gay marriage, which history finally forced her to renounce in 2013, was part political calculation, part Midwestern Methodist.

Hillary cast her vote for the Iraq War without having read the full National Intelligence Estimate, which was far more skeptical about Iraq's weaponry than the bowdlerized version that was made public. This was very strange behavior for someone as disciplined as Hillary, famous for working late and taking a stack of briefing books home. Senator Bob Graham, one of the few who actually did take the trouble to read the NIE, voted against the war in part because of what it contained. We can never know why she chose not to read the document, but it's hard not to conclude that she wanted to vote for war more than she wanted to know the truth.

Hillary even accused Saddam of having ties to al-Qaeda—essentially siding with Bush and Cheney to a degree that no other Democrat, even Joe Lieberman, approached. Most of Bill's foreign policy advisors rejected such a position as nonsense. Kenneth

Pollack, a prowar National Security Council veteran who'd also advised Hillary, told Gerth and Van Natta that the Saddam/al-Qaeda link was "bullshit.... We all knew that was bullshit."[85] It took Hillary years to admit her vote was a "mistake." After the war went sour, Hillary argued that the Bush administration hadn't pursued diplomatic approaches fervently enough—even though she voted against an amendment that would have required the president to do just that before any invasion.[86]

Another vote Hillary now regrets is the one she cast in favor of the 2001 bankruptcy reform bill. Big finance had been lobbying to reverse American law's traditional indulgence of debtors for years. They wanted to make it much harder for people with onerous credit card debt to "discharge" it—have it wiped away forever—by a fairly simple bankruptcy filing. They finally got one through Congress at the very end of Bill's presidency. It was mostly written, Elizabeth Warren told me back when she was still a professor at Harvard Law School, by a law firm for the credit card industry, Morrison & Foerster of San Francisco. (The firm is nicknamed, and uses as its internet domain, "MoFo." Not your usual elite legal *politesse*.)

Hillary asked Warren to brief her on the bill. Warren, a long-standing opponent of creditor-friendly bankruptcy reform, quickly convinced her that it was a horror that would hurt poor and middle-income people badly, single mothers prominently among them. Hillary went back to the White House and lobbied her husband to veto the bill. He did—it was one of the last acts of his term in office, along with pardoning Marc Rich. [87]

Two years later, though, Hillary was in the Senate, "representing Wall Street," as she reminded us in the first 2015 Democratic debate. Another version of bankruptcy reform came up and this time, forgetting everything she learned from Warren, Hillary voted for it. When asked to explain the vote during the 2015 campaign she said that enough changes had been made to the bill to justify her vote—a position almost none of the anti-bankruptcy reform advocates took—and then pointedly noted that then-senator Joe Biden, a dear friend of the credit card industry who was once known as the senator from MBNA (a major card issuer based in Biden's home state of Delaware, now part of Bank of America), urged her to vote for it.[88] Now that Biden isn't running, she probably won't do this again, but you never know.

But other than warmongering, defending creditors, and eagerly making friends with the opposition, her Senatorial accomplishments were minimal. Hilary Bok, a professor at Johns Hopkins who used to blog under the name "hilzoy," compiled a list of the successful bills that Hillary had sponsored; they were mostly about minor issues such as the renaming of post offices in the memory of local worthies or the use of low-energy lightbulbs in public buildings. A couple of her bills promoted the use of electric vehicles and the use of heat pumps to conserve modest amounts of energy.[89] Alarmed by "a silent epidemic" of "pornographic and violent" games, she urged an investigation of the video game industry by the Federal Trade Commission and also introduced a bill to tighten regulations on the sale of "mature" video games to minors. It went nowhere.[90] (In *It Takes a Village*, she praised the work of Tipper Gore and William Bennett against gangsta rap and decried the pervasive violence of popular culture; unsurprisingly she didn't apply this critique of violence to her foreign policy preferences.)[91] She also cosponsored a bill to criminalize burning the American flag, a strategy she saw as a compromise between those who think flag-burning is a form of free speech and those who want a constitutional amendment to ban it.[92]

A survey on Congress.gov of the legislation she sponsored or cosponsored provides further evidence of its profound insubstantiality: a resolution "honoring the victims of the bombing of Pan Am flight 103," a bill to allow taxpayers to designate a portion of their refunds to help homeless veterans, a bill to require country of origin labels on dairy products, and so on. Few of these bills went anywhere. Almost all of her Senate record, the Iraq vote aside, was the legislative equivalent of being against cancer. In fact, she introduced a resolution expressing "support for the goals and ideals of Pancreatic Cancer Awareness Month."[93] You just can't argue with that.

Hillary voted against an amendment to the 2007 military appropriations bill that would have sharply restricted the use of cluster bombs in areas with any "concentrated population of civilians, whether permanent or temporary." The amendment was introduced by Sen. Diane Feinstein—no softie—who said this in its support:

> Cluster munitions are large bombs, rockets, or artillery shells that contain up to hundreds of small submunitions or individual bomblets. They are intended for attacking enemy troop formations and armor, covering approximately a .6-mile radius.... [T]hey pose a real threat to the safety of civilians when used in populated areas because they leave hundreds of unexploded bombs over a very large area and they are often inaccurate.... [I]n some cases, up to 40 percent of cluster bombs fail to explode, posing a particular danger to civilians long after the conflict has ended. This is particularly and sadly true of children.... They pick [cluster bombs] up out of curiosity because they look like balls and they start playing with them and a terrible result follows.

According to Feinstein, 11,000 people, almost a third of them children, have been killed by leftover cluster bombs since the

1960s in Southeast Asia. In Iraq, 1,600 civilians have been killed by leftover munitions dropped during the First Gulf War.

The amendment failed by a 70–30 vote. All 30 yes votes were from Democrats. The nays came from every Republican, 55 of them, and 15 Dems, Hillary included.

But, true to her instinct for the small noncontroversial gesture, Hillary co-sponsored an amendment to the same appropriation bill to authorize the spending of an additional $12 million for the Defense and Veterans Brain Injury Center. Hard to argue with, unlike cluster bombs.[94]

When faced with a challenge from the left—when they're not in redbaiting mode, that is—Hillary fans like to counter that her voting record in the Senate was among the most liberal during her time in that body, and that it was virtually identical to Sanders'. What they don't tell you is that some of the votes that she and Sanders differed on were rather important. In a review of their records, Derek Willis of the *New York Times* says that "the 31 times that Mrs. Clinton and Mr. Sanders disagreed happened to be on some [of] the biggest issues of the day, including measures on continuing the wars in Iraq and Afghanistan, an immigration reform bill and bank bailouts during the depths of the Great Recession." Sanders voted no on all of these. Sanders' vote against the immigration reform bill was based on concerns about exploitative guest worker programs; many immigrant advocates and unions opposed it for those reasons.[95]

PLANNING FOR THE FUTURE

Hillary ran her Senate office in a manner that those accustomed to her way of working would easily recognize: secretively and with a penchant for skirting rules. She'd begun building the world now widely known as "Hillaryland" during her time as First Lady, and by the time she got to the Senate it was well established. Its inhabitants were, and still are, a tight circle of confidants and advisors, tight-lipped and intensely loyal to the boss. As a Senate source said to Gerth and Van Natta, "If you are disloyal or indiscreet, there will be a price for the disloyalty. There is a fear of retribution that permeates the group." Hillary used Senate email servers for political fundraising, which is illegal, and kept a few dozen employees as "congressional fellows," off the books and outside the realm of public accountability (a practice she continued as Secretary of State, as we'll see).[96]

During her Senate years, Hillary spent her spare time building a formidable political machine—a loyal circle of advisors, a PAC, and, with help from others, a think tank and media operation. The think tank, the Center for American Progress (CAP), was founded in 2003 by Bill's former chief of staff, John Podesta (chair of Hillary's 2016 campaign), in conjunction with other members of the Clinton inner circle and Democratic moneybags like George Soros. In a 2004 article on CAP's early history, Robert Dreyfuss described it as "a shadow government, a kind of Clinton White-House-in-exile—or a White House staff in readiness for President Hillary Clinton." It was founded very much in the New Democrat mode, safely centrist, tough on defense and incremental on domestic policy, with an approach distinctly unlike the ideological warriors who staffed Heritage and Cato from their early days.[97] (It's now repositioning itself as deeply concerned about inequality, as if the finance-friendly free-trading New Dems had nothing to do with causing the problem.)

Unlike most major think tanks, which issue annual reports with helpful information about their patrons, CAP has long resisted disclosing its donors. The investigative journalist Ken Silverstein obtained internal documentation showing generous funding from Comcast, Wal-Mart, GE, Boeing, and Lockheed.[98] CAP grudgingly revealed some donor info in January 2015. Among the big names: the Gates Foundation, the United Arab Emirates, Apple, Blackstone, Citigroup, Goldman Sachs… Many names, however, remained anonymous.[99]

The media machine took the form of David Brock's Media Matters for America (MMfA), founded in 2004, an apparently independent operation run by a madly loyal operative. (CAP gave it office space in its early days.) Like CAP, the organization has resisted releasing names of its supporters, but in 2010 Soros disclosed that he'd just donated a million dollars.[100] Among the earlier funders was the Democracy Alliance, a consortium of liberal plutocrats (which also gave to CAP), Soros among them.[101] Although MMfA fights against press attacks on all Democrats, Hillary has long been their special cause. That bias is no accident: in a 2007 speech, she bragged about "the new progressive infrastructure—institutions that I helped to start and support like Media Matters and Center for American Progress."[102]

Democrats used to complain about the Republican use of dark money, secret piles of cash gathered unaccountably for partisan ends. Now that the Clintons have mastered the art, you don't hear those complaints anymore except from the margins. Meanwhile, this richly funded institution-building left Hillary well positioned for a presidential run.

4 FIRST TRY

Though she deliberated for years about whether to run for president, Hillary's 2008 campaign started out with the same descriptor as that of her 2016 run: she was an "inevitable winner." The rise of Barack Obama eventually proved that this was far from the truth, frustrating her plan to win heavily in the early contests and deal a fatal blow to any impertinent competition. A political psychoanalyst might suspect that constant assertions of inevitability are a defense mechanism designed to counter a candidate's deep vulnerability. But Hillary did look like a sure bet in the early days of the campaign. Her inner circle viewed Obama as a "phenomenon," a glittering bauble that could easily be smashed. Yes, there was John Edwards, but a combination of over-attention to haircuts and mistresses soon disposed of him.

Obama's image as an "outsider," an Iraq War opponent, and a former community organizer gave him what in retrospect looks like an unwarranted insurgent appeal. His outsiderhood was, of course, grossly exaggerated: groomed by elites since his youth, he was urged to run for president by Harry Reid after less than two years in the Senate. Reid could see that Obama didn't have the gregarious, deal-making temperament necessary for success in the upper chamber, and thought that he'd be a bright alternative to Hillary. To Reid and other senior Dems, Hillary held too much risk of electoral catastrophe. Her vote for the Iraq War was toxic to the party's left, and the campaign would revive memories of all the old Clinton scandals. Washington was abuzz with rumors that Bill was still on the prowl (as is Chappaqua today). Republican opposition researchers, it was felt, would make merry with all of it, and the party would get crushed in the election.[103]

Obama was a phenomenon indeed, but one that was not easily crushed. He was something of a blank screen onto which millions could project their fantasies of a more peaceful, more egalitarian world. Checks poured into his campaign. When the first quarter fundraising results were released in April 2007, Hillary's people were shocked to learn that he'd brought in more cash than she had, and from a far broader array of donors.[104] She still led in the polls, but the race tightened as the year went on. Despite a "likability tour," an initiative whose name says it all, she did badly in the Iowa caucuses in early January 2008, causing serious damage to her aura of inevitability.[105] After that defeat, New Hampshire looked bad, but she pulled off a surprising victory there. She suffered a serious blow in South Carolina in late

January, where the black vote was decisive (more on that below). She did fairly well on Super Tuesday in early February, roughly splitting the delegate haul with Obama. In late February, her anxiety growing, she unleashed the sensational "3 AM ad," which implied that Obama was too inexperienced to handle a national security crisis arising in the middle of the night, a weakness that would place the nation's children at risk.[106] In March, she famously invented the story of landing under sniper fire in Bosnia in 1996, a claim that she retracted a week later.[107] By May, despite occasional energetic performances of "populism," her campaign was limping along, short on cash and prospects. It was all over in early June.

Hillary fought hard to the end, but closed her campaign $25 million in debt, a humiliating finish for a candidate who'd been almost universally regarded as the presumptive nominee just a year earlier.[108]

Although Hillary led among black voters early in the 2008 campaign, that changed with increasing exposure to Obama. She deployed some nasty race-baiting rhetoric to try to counteract this. Speaking to *USA Today* reporters after a pair of damaging primary losses in May 2008, she said that "Senator Obama's support among working, hard-working Americans, white Americans, is weakening again," thereby hinting at ancient tropes about black laziness and their lack of real Americanness.[109] (She never went as far as her pollster/strategist Mark Penn recommended, however. He wanted her to miss no opportunity to emphasize that Obama was "not at his center fundamentally American in his thinking and in his values.")[110] Her husband, no stranger to race-play himself, disparaged Obama as reminiscent of "a gifted television commentator," and explained his victory in the South Carolina primary in January 2008 by pointing out that Jesse Jackson won the state in 1984 and 1988, an unsubtle reminder that the state was the second-blackest in the country in 1980 and the third in 1990.[111] Bill also complained that "they played the race card on me. We now know, from memos from the campaign that they planned to do it all along." It looked like the Clinton strategy was to turn Obama from a black candidate into the black candidate.[112] Amy Chozick, a *New York Times* reporter on the Hillary beat who often sounds like her publicist, noting her call for more of a national conversation on race—talk is fine, as long as the action doesn't get too redistributive—conceded that "she wrestled uncomfortably in competing against the man who would become the first black president." Her husband's comments during the campaign, Chozick added, "seemed to diminish Mr. Obama's stature."[113] "Aimed to" might be more accurate than "seemed to."

(One should never forget almost-2016-candidate Joe Biden's shining moment from the 2008 campaign, when he said of Obama: "I mean, you got the first mainstream African-American who is articulate and bright and clean and a nice-looking guy. I mean, that's a storybook, man." Biden later apologized, claimed his remarks were taken out of context, and claimed his usage of "clean" was innocently derived from his mother's.)[114]

Many reasons were given for Hillary's loss in 2008, notably infighting among her staff, reckless spending habits, and a general indiscipline. But the more fundamental reason was that she was never as magnetic a candidate as her rival. Aside from disagreements over the Iraq War, the policy differences between Hillary and Obama were minimal; he was just more appealing as a person than she was.

More appealing and, he hoped, less divisive. Transcending divisiveness is one of the dreams of centrists, as if disagreement were a bad habit rather than fundamental to politics. In one of the early debates, Obama accused Hillary of being too partisan a figure, precisely the candidate that Republicans would love to face:

Part of the reason that Republicans...are obsessed with you, Hillary, is that's a fight they're very comfortable having. It is the fight that we've been through since the nineties. And part of the job of the next president is to break the gridlock and get Democrats and independents and Republicans to start working together to solve big problems, like health care or climate change or energy. And what we don't need is another eight years of bickering.[115]

You have to wonder if Obama believed this when he said it, though he tried to govern that way for much of his time in office, seeking compromise with a party that wanted to destroy him. It was an especially curious line of argument given that Hillary had spent so much of her Senate career buddying up to Republicans.

Despite considerable bad feeling toward her in his camp (which reportedly lingers to this day), a victorious Obama named Hillary to the office of Secretary of State. This prompted references to Lincoln's "cabinet of rivals," a triumph of coalition-building, but to many it looked more like a way of keeping a potential rival busy for the coming years.

5 DIPLOMAT

Hillary had few accomplishments as a diplomat, but her tenure as Secretary of State was a great time for the Clinton philanthropies.

Let's turn first to partisan accounts of Hillary's achievements as Secretary of State, presumably the strongest case for her tenure. A July 2014 visit to the website of Correct the Record, a pro-Hillary organization run by her former-enemy-turned-promoter David Brock, offered typically vapid fluff on its front page: "In this world and the world of tomorrow, we must go forward together or not at all." It also informs us that Hillary traveled 956,733 miles as Secretary of State.[116] The testimony to her peripatetic vigor was linked to a list of her alleged accomplishments at State, which included:

- helping to restore American "leadership and standing in the world," though the only metrics offered to support this are the miles logged and meetings taken with "foreign leaders in 112 countries"

- helping to impose the toughest sanctions on Iran in history
- helping to avoid all-out war in Gaza
- working "to build the coalition to oust Qadhafi [sic] and stop massacres in Libya"
- developing the "'pivot to Asia' strategy," which "will probably be Obama's most lasting strategic achievement" (the details of which are left undisclosed)
- negotiating free-trade agreements with Colombia, Panama, and South Korea
- and, elevating the cause of women's rights

In the years that followed, Israel assaulted Gaza (killing, by B'Tselem's count, 1,764 Palestinians),[117] Obama reached a nuclear deal with Iran (which Hillary publicly supported, though in a truculent way, trying to sound hawkish without sounding disloyal), and Libya turned into a wreck. Free-trade agreements are not the kind of thing that gets the non–Wall Street base excited. Elevating the cause of women's rights is certainly laudable, but seems not to have changed much in what the website elsewhere called "deeply reactionary cultures," which are presumably located only abroad. As for America's standing in the world, Pew polls show that the initial bounce in the U.S. image abroad that came with Obama's election eroded, substantially in some countries—and

Hillary was particularly disliked in predominantly Muslim nations.[118]

Other partisan efforts by fans to talk up her diplomatic accomplishments fall ludicrously short. Writing for *Policy.Mic*, Eli Sugarman touted her "people-to-people diplomacy," the promotion of business opportunities for U.S. corporations abroad (especially for foundation donors, but Sugarman didn't mention them), "restoring American credibility" (however that is measured), the promotion of military force in Pakistan and Libya (how diplomatic), and, no kidding, the rampant success of "texts from Hillary" memes.[119]

Mainstream press evaluations of Hillary's time at State show a competent but unspectacular record. Writing in the *Los Angeles Times*, Paul Richter reported that she "devoted long hours to signature issues, including empowerment of women and girls, gay rights, Third World development, health and Internet freedoms."[120] It's difficult to trace much progress resulting from Hillary's long hours, however. She was involved in no diplomatic initiatives of note, and left no mark on strategy. She worked with David Petraeus, former general turned CIA director, on a plan to arm the Syrian rebels—for a diplomat, she was in love with warriors, frequently advocating military approaches in Cabinet meetings—but the White House never bought the plan.[121]

On the academic end, Harvard international relations professor Stephen Walt acknowledged that while she had some accomplishments, like improving the morale of the Foreign Service after the dismal Bush years, she didn't do much otherwise—in large part because Obama didn't want her to do much.[122] Numerous sources describe Obama running foreign policy largely from the White House, leaving State out of the loop.

EMAILS

One of the outstanding features of Hillary's time at State wouldn't be revealed for several years after she left office: her private email server. As is now widely known, before taking office, she arranged to have her electronic correspondence run though a server in the family's Chappaqua house instead of the official State Department server. The domain "clintonemail.com," was registered on the very day of her Senate confirmation hearing.[123] (It's interesting that she chose "hdr22@clintonemail.com" as her address. Presumably "hdr" stands for her premarital name, Hillary Diane Rodham. No Clinton. The "22" part is the subject of much internet speculation but its meaning remains unknown. Would *Catch-22* be too obvious?)

Coincidentally, the State Department had no permanent inspector general for her entire tenure—the longest gap since the position was created in 1957. The Office of the Inspector General serves as an in-house auditor, reviewing the effectiveness, efficiency, and legality of Department operations.[124] Acting inspectors, like the one in place during her time at State, are generally regarded as less serious auditors than permanent ones.[125]

In an email to supporters, Hillary claimed that she did nothing wrong by using a private server, and that its use was "above board." The claim is hard to accept for anyone familiar with her history. Given the timing of the domain registration, it's difficult not to believe that she knew exactly what she was doing—keeping her emails safe from outside scrutiny. Hillary is nothing if not a meticulous planner. Her husband's major scandal was about a blow job; hers, from the days of the Rose Law Firm onward, have often derived from her feeling that rules are for the little people, especially if they threaten her desire to keep things hidden.

When a judge ordered the release of the emails, Hillary deleted over 30,000 of them—because, according to her, they were mostly personal trivia, like "yoga routines" and plans for her daughter Chelsea's wedding.[126] Considering that among those she did release was a request to an aide to fetch her an iced tea, you do have to wonder what was in the deleted ones.

The emails, heavily redacted and released only in install-ments, make for entertaining reading. Among other things, they reveal that she suffered serious status anxiety. Since, as was noted earlier, Obama largely conducted foreign policy from the White House, Hillary's room for maneuver was sharply limited. This evidently bothered her a great deal. She lamented that she saw Obama only once a week, in contrast with Henry Kissinger, who met with Nixon every day. (In a review of Kissinger's chilling-ly titled *World Order*, she praised his "breadth and acuity" and described him as "a friend," on whose "counsel" she relied while Secretary of State. Her appreciation of her predecessor seems apt. There's something reminiscent of Kissinger about Hillary—the ruthlessness, the admiration of toughness and force, the pen-chant for deception and secrecy, the view of diplomacy as war continued by other means.) She also obsessed about not being invited to the right meetings, and wondered if Obama and his closer associates held grudges against her and her posse after the nasty 2008 primary.[127]

Some emails she chose not to release have come to light. For example, she failed to turn over nine complete emails and parts of six others in which she was shown to be encouraging longtime Clinton family advisor Sidney Blumenthal to continue reporting on Libya. Her official story was that his advice was "unsolicit-ed," but the emails suggest anything but.[128] In one, she wrote to

Blumenthal, "thanks for keeping this stuff coming!" The Clinton Foundation was paying Blumenthal $10,000 a month while he was volunteering this advice. A Hillary flack nonetheless told the *New York Times* that "the idea that this runs counter to the assertion that the emails were unsolicited is a leap."[129]

The neo-populist Hillary of 2015 is a long way from the banker-flattering Secretary of State revealed by her emails. She urged her staff to help an associate of private equity (PE) titan Steven Schwarzman—the man with the biggest living room in Manhattan, a major fundraiser for George W. Bush, and a $250,000 contributor to the Clinton Foundation—to get a visa. Schwarzman once said of an Obama administration proposal to lift the "carried interest" tax break enjoyed by PE managers that "it's like when Hitler invaded Poland in 1939."[130] She had a warm correspondence with Terrence Duffy, head of the CME Group (parent of the Chicago Mercantile Exchange CME, the giant futures market) and a fervent supporter in the 2008 campaign.[131]

(Hillary has an interesting history with futures markets— recall her brilliant trading in cattle contracts, which are listed on the CME, that turned $1,000 into $100,000 back during her Little Rock days. Far more common are people who begin with $100,000 and end with $1,000. Her trading was done with the advice of her friend James Blair, who was also outside counsel to Tyson Foods, an entity that had heavy dealings with the state of Arkansas. Although Hillary, a total novice, claimed she made the trading decisions herself, records show that Blair entered the orders. The cash in her account was frequently allowed to go below regulatory limits. No one has been able to prove anything illegal or unethical in the trading, but near 100-fold returns are extremely unusual. There were significant discrepancies between the trading records that the White House initially released when the story came to light in 1994 and those obtained from the CME. The CME's records, the *Washington Post* reported, "raise the possibility that some of her profits…came from larger trades ordered by someone else and then shifted to her account.")[132]

We can expect her to forget these warm attachments to the likes of Schwarzman and Duffy when she fights on behalf of "everyday Americans."

HILLARYLAND AT FOGGY BOTTOM

Running the State Department provided Hillary with rich opportunities for patronage, especially in the hiring of old friends and associates to well-paid positions. She was a heavy user of Special Government Employee (SGE) status, which allows staffers to escape normal conflict-of-interest scrutiny. The category is generally reserved for temporary positions being filled by outside experts, but in a manner reminiscent of Hillary's Senate personnel practices, she used it at State for longer-term hires. The most prominent of her SGEs was Huma Abedin, who is now the vice-chair of her presidential campaign. Abedin started working for Hillary in 1996, while still a college student, and was employed later on her 2008 campaign.

While she was advising the nation's top diplomat, Abedin moonlighted, like many Americans, by working for Teneo, a consulting firm founded by Doug Band—longtime advisor to Bill, and a major force in creating his post-presidential philanthropist/promoter enterprise. She was also hired as a consultant to the Clinton Foundation itself.[133]

When Abedin's SGE status was first reported by *Politico, ProPublica* filed a Freedom of Information Act request to get a full list of Hillary's SGEs. Two months after the filing, State, while confirming that there were about 100 such employees, protested that compiling a full list would be too difficult to complete. When *ProPublica* said it would do a story on their refusal, the Department came up with the list—five months after the first request. It included Caitlin Klevorick, who ran a consulting firm that counted among its clients "Fortune 100 companies" (according to her own PR material). "Should a consultant to giant multinationals also be working at the State Department?" is a question that is both rhetorical and of substance. Hillary also used SGE status to provide employment to her longtime sidekick Cheryl Mills (who was Klevorick's boss), as well as Maggie Williams, who ran her 2008 campaign.[134]

With Abedin and Klevorick, as Craig Holman of Public Citizen told *ProPublica,* "There is a very high potential for actual conflicts of interest in this case, and…certainly every appearance of conflicts of interest." The cases of Mills and Williams are interesting studies in the construction of Hillaryland, her circle of loyalists who've surrounded her for years. Public jobs, foundation jobs, campaign jobs—it's all reminiscent of Wallace Stevens' phrase "the pleasures of merely circulating."

Doug Band's story, though a minor detour in a book about Hillary, is worth recounting. Band became Bill's body man—carrying bags, keeping track of time, fetching Cokes—late in Bill's presidency and stayed on staff afterward. His responsibilities expanded and he ended up joining Bill as he jetted around with billionaires such as supermarket magnate Ron Burkle, whose private jet earned the nickname "Air Fuck One" for all its reputed onboard cavorting. One day at the World Economic Forum's annual meeting in Davos, with CEOs lining up to meet his boss, the idea struck Band that Bill could juice up the languishing philanthropy he'd founded in 2001 with similar conferences, where the rich and their courtiers could network.

And so, in 2005, the Clinton Global Initiative (CGI) was born. As Alec McGinnis, in an excellent article on Band, put it, "CGI operates like an economy in which celebrity is the main currency." Get the right people together, and with the help of money, projects can be undertaken. And they were.

Some of the contributors Band brought into the Foundation's orbit were less than wholesome. There was Victor Dahdaleh, a London-based businessman, who gave $5 million to the Foundation in 2010 and was indicted a year later for bribery. And there was Raffaello Follieri, a young Italian operator who buddied up to Band with promises of contributions to the Foundation. They lived the high life together for a while until Follieri was unmasked as a fraud and ended up in federal prison. These associations, and Band's heavy trading on his relationship with Bill, led to worries that Band was besmirching the Clinton brand. His arrogance didn't win him any friends either.

Along with two partners, Band started Teneo in 2011, a consulting firm that sold its services to big capital, and included on its board not only Bill but also Tony Blair. Many of its clients happened to be Clinton Foundation contributors. Band's greediness in working the Clinton connection finally got to be too much for Bill, and Band was shown the door in 2012. Throughout the period that Band's extravagance was causing distress in the Clinton camp, Huma Abedin was one of his staunchest allies.[135]

Despite the split of its chief with Clinton, Band's company Teneo continues to do well for itself, managing several major acquisitions and earning backing from a private equity firm.[136] It has over 500 "professionals" operating in 14 cities around the world. By its own description, it

> partners exclusively with the CEOs and senior leaders of many of the world's largest and most complex companies and organizations. The firm is focused on working with clients to address a wide range of financial, reputational and transformational challenges and opportunities by combining the disciplines of strategic communications, investor relations, investment banking, financial analytics, executive recruiting, digital analytics, corporate governance, government affairs, business intelligence, management consulting and corporate restructuring on an integrated basis.[137]

The Clinton circle can be truly magical indeed.

PIVOT TO ASIA

Insofar as Hillary had a strategic vision as Secretary of State, it was her "pivot to Asia," later rebranded as a "rebalance," that she outlined in a 2011 article for *Foreign Policy*.[138] In her memoir of her diplomatic career, *Hard Choices*, Hillary said the goal was to assert American power, previously so focused on the Middle East, in the Pacific—without "an unnecessary confrontation with China." Her *FP* essay was a call for an expansion of U.S. imperial ambitions in the Pacific, against those citizens who would "come home" after the ravages of the Iraq and Afghanistan wars. After a war goes badly, the political class always has to talk the public out of wanting to give up on the whole foreign entanglements game. Hillary's pivot would feature "forward-deployed" diplomacy and "a broad-based military presence." It's striking how militarized her diplomatic strategies could be. Much of the article was devoted to talking up trade agreements, notably the Trans-Pacific Partnership (TPP), which is really more a bill of rights for capital than a trade agreement, and an unusual concern for a Secretary of State. With most Democrats opposing the TPP, especially the more liberal ones who vote in primaries, Hillary came out against the TPP in September 2015, despite having played a large role in negotiating and promoting it.

The diplomatic achievements of the pivot are hard to name. Outside the diplomatic process, the United States has been engaging in a substantial military buildup in the Pacific—a buildup the Chinese have used to justify their own escalation.[139] Though the Chinese economy is slowing, and could contract sharply, China will continue to build its global influence. Washington may not like China's increasing military presence in the South China Sea, but there's not much it can do about it. A U.S. naval buildup won't mean much if the Chinese know the Americans would never dare to attack. Washington may be bellicose, but it knows well enough to pick weak enemies.

The turn to Asia did, however, provide the best line in *Hard Choices*. As Hillary herself reports it, in the midst of tough negotiations, the Chinese official, Dai Bingguo, posed a question to the Secretary of State: "Why don't you 'pivot' out of here?"[140]

MEXICAN OIL

Hillary's interest in the economic aspects of diplomacy went well beyond the TPP. According to investigative journalist Steve Horn, Hillary worked to open up the Mexican oil and gas sector—previously a nationalist preserve—to foreign oil companies, particularly American ones. A milestone in this opening was the granting of drilling rights in the Gulf of Mexico to foreign bidders with the December 2013 signing of the U.S.–Mexico Transboundary Agreement. That agreement, in the words of the official U.S. government release, "establishes a framework for U.S.

offshore oil and gas companies and Mexico's Petroleos Mexicanos (PEMEX) to jointly develop" oil reservoirs that straddled the U.S.–Mexico boundary.[141] One of the key figures in the initiative, Carlos Pascual, who was Ambassador to Mexico from 2009–2011 and later the State Department's top energy honcho, outlined the political strategy in a WikiLeaks cable that Horn quotes:

> Publicly, the GOM [government of Mexico] will emphasize that the negotiations allow Mexico to defend its natural resources. [Energy Secretary Georgia] Kessel explained the sensitivity of energy issues in Mexico, noting that many Mexicans consider oil a part of the country's DNA…while the GOM will portray negotiations on trans-boundary reservoirs to the Mexican public as an effort to defend the country's natural resources, the government sees a treaty as an important opportunity for PEMEX [the Mexican national oil company] to work with IOCs [international oil companies] and gain expertise in deepwater drilling. For the first time in decades, the door to the USG's constructive engagement with Mexico on oil has opened a crack. It would be in our interests to take advantage of this opportunity.

This opening—more than a crack—has been a long-standing

dream of Big Oil, and Hillary's diplomacy helped it to come true. It doesn't speak well of her environmental commitments, though: deepwater drilling is a risky, filthy business. (Fortunately, the collapse in oil prices has, at least for now, put a damper on industry enthusiasm for the technique.) But the maneuvering did pay off for three of her top aides on the Mexican oil-opening project— they went on to lucrative jobs in the energy business and energy think tanks.[142]

HONDURAS

While the diplomatic work in Mexico was innovative, Hillary's work in Honduras was along more traditional lines—supporting a coup against the elected leftish government of Manuel Zelaya. Zelaya, who emerged from the country's elite, moved left while in office, raising social spending, allying with popular movements, and signing agreements with Hugo Chavez's Venezuela. In June 2009, the Honduran army ousted Zelaya and drove him into exile. The coup was widely condemned, though not so much in Washington. Publicly, the United States expressed discomfort, without ever sounding emphatic, while refusing to use the word "coup" to describe what had occurred.[143]

But, as a batch of released emails shows, Hillary was privately moving to keep Zelaya from returning to office. To help in this deception, she proposed using longtime Clinton family fixer Lanny Davis—a lobbyist whose client list includes for-profit colleges and the kleptocratic, murderous dictator of Equatorial Guinea—as a back channel to the interim president installed after the coup. [144] Coincidentally, Davis—who once gushed to Hillary in an email that, aside from his family, she was "the best friend and the best person I have met in my long life"—had been hired by the Honduran Business Council to sell the coup in the United States.[145]

An election designed to legitimate the coup, which was widely condemned as fraudulent across the southern hemisphere, was effusively endorsed by the State Department's chief negotiator for the Honduras talks. Zelaya—whom Hillary described in *Hard Choices* as "a throwback to the caricature of a Central American strongman"—was never returned to office. In her memoir, she lamented the coup as the return of "the ghosts of Latin America's troubled past," touted her concern for the well-being of Zelaya's family, and declared that she "didn't see any choice but to condemn Zelaya's ouster." Supporting it privately, though, was OK—as was celebrating the coup's aftermath as a "victory for democracy."[146]

(As the journalist Belén Fernández discovered, Hillary deleted her [dishonest] account of the Honduran coup from the paperback version of *Hard Choices*.)[147]

It was all a deeply cynical performance. Greg Grandin, a historian who specializes in Latin America, puts it this way:

> Her emails show that early on in the 2009 coup against Manuel Zelaya, when there was a real chance of restoring the reformist president to his office, she was working with the most retrograde elements in Honduras to consolidate the putsch. Let's be clear: grassroots Democrats who support Clinton for president would be enormously sympathetic to the coalition that was trying to reverse the Honduras coup, comprised of environmentalists, LBGT activists, people trying to make the morning-after pill available, progressive religious folks, anti-mining and anti-biofuel peasants, and legal reformers working to humanize Honduras' lethal police–prison regime. And Clinton betrayed them, serving them up to Honduras' crime-ridden oligarchy. Hundreds of good people have since been murdered by the people Clinton sided with in late 2009 and early 2010.[148]

Among those murdered was the indigenous rights and environmental activist Berta Cáceres, who was killed on March 3, 2016. We don't know who exactly pulled the trigger, but the killer(s) certainly sprang from the forces that Greg Grandin describes above.

In a 2014 interview, Cáceres condemned Hillary for legitimating the coup: "The same Hillary Clinton, in her book *Hard Choices*, practically said what was going to happen in Honduras. This demonstrates the bad legacy of North American influence in our country…. We warned that this would be very dangerous…. The elections took place under intense militarism, and enormous fraud."[149] These are the elections that Hillary said would make everything OK.

HAITI

No review of Hillary's diplomatic career would be complete without an examination of her work in Haiti. Bill and Hillary have a rich shared history with the country, one of the poorest in the world. (Its per capita annual income is equal to about twelve seconds of their standard speaking fee.)[150] During Hillary's Secretaryship, she and Bill were, as a *Politico* headline put it, "The King and Queen of Haiti."[151]

Their history with Haiti began with a 1975 trip—a leg of an extended honeymoon—to Port-au-Prince that was financed by David Edwards, an old friend of Bill's who was working for Citibank and who had some business to transact in the country. [152] In his memoir, Bill claimed that Edwards used his frequent-flyer miles to pay for the trip, but frequent-flyer programs didn't begin until airline deregulation hit in 1979 and the junket looks like the first of many sponsored journeys to come. You have to hand it to them: their first date involved crossing a picket line, and their honeymoon was a banker-financed trip to the Caribbean.

On that first trip, the newlyweds and Edwards went to a voodoo ceremony conducted by a Sorbonne alum, during which a man walked across burning coals and a woman bit the head off a live chicken. In his strangely abrupt accounting of the sequence in his memoirs, Bill, fresh from an electoral defeat, emerged from the experience resolving to run for attorney general back in Arkansas, because of something the ceremony taught him about how "the Lord works in mysterious ways."[153]

Many years later, early in his presidency, Bill engineered the return to office of Jean-Bertrand Aristide, who had been elected as president of Haiti in 1990 as a serious progressive reformer and was promptly overthrown in a coup. The army's subsequent rule was predictably brutal, but the Bush administration was fine with the arrangement, since it saw eye-to-eye with the rapacious

Haitian elite. Bill was troubled, however, and when he took office he began maneuvering for a restoration of Aristide. A UN resolution in 1994 authorized a U.S.-led military force to restore Aristide to office, earning Bill plaudits as a friend of democracy. But the restoration was conditional on the acceptance of an IMF-written austerity and privatization program, which largely eviscerated Aristide's reformist agenda.[154] You could consider this an early instance of the left wing of neoliberalism, with the Bush position representing its right. Either way you get rule by a moneyed elite, but the left variety is more attentive to optics.

On becoming Secretary of State, Hillary resolved to make Haiti a foreign policy priority. It was to be a prime example of a new development strategy that would, as Jonathan Katz put it in a detailed history of the couple's relationship with the country, put "business at its center: Aid would be replaced by investment, the growth of which would in turn benefit the United States."[155]

Promoting foreign investment often requires keeping wages low, which is precisely what Hillary's State Department successfully helped engineer, as a series of WikiLeaks cables published by *The Nation* and *Haïti Liberté* revealed. When the Haitian parliament unanimously passed an increase in the minimum wage to $5 a day—an amount that Hillary earned in about 0.07 seconds at her standard speaking fee—U.S. business interests on the island mobilized. President René Préval, who had replaced Aristide, then engineered a two-tiered compromise minimum. The U.S. Embassy was not pleased, dismissing the president's move as a "populist measure aimed at appealing to 'the unemployed and underpaid masses.'"[156] Rising to the defense of this brutal reasoning, Adam Davidson, host of NPR's Planet Money—who portrayed himself in an interview with me as having grown up in a bohemian West Village culture, and who cultivates the image that he's cooler than his econobeat would suggest—explained that to earn $5 a day, Haitians would simply have to develop the skills to perform complex tasks.[157]

The WikiLeaks cables also showed the U.S. State Department collaborating in 2009 with other Western Hemisphere ambassadors to push ahead with corrupt elections from which the country's largest party, Aristide's Fanmi Lavalas (FL), was excluded. The elections were delayed by the January 2010 earthquake. When they were eventually held, they were a disgrace, with fraud rampant, and a 23% turnout.[158] Michel "Sweet Micky" Martelly, a singer and supporter of the second coup against Aristide (mounted in 2004), was proclaimed the winner by the Organization of American States, with Hillary Clinton presiding.

The cynicism around the election was perfectly captured in an email from Hillary's longtime aide Cheryl Mills, who wrote this to the Port-au-Prince embassy staff on March 20, 2011, the night of the runoff that delivered Martelly his victory:

Nice job. Nice job all. You do great elections. And make us all look good. I am so very grateful for all you have done. Dinner on me in Haiti next trip. [And we can discuss how the counting is going! Just kidding. Kinda. :)][159]

Evidently the counting was no straightforward affair; official results weren't announced until a month later, on April 21. They were greeted with protests across the country. In an account of Hillary's history with Haiti, *New York Times* reporter Yamiche Alicindor quoted Mills' email, adding, with the paper's characteristic patronizing tone, that "it has fed a suspicion among Haitians, if lacking in proof, that the United States rigged the election to install a puppet president."[160] Those Haitians will believe anything.

Soon after his selection, Martelly appointed Bill Clinton to an advisory board to encourage foreign investment in the country.[161] There wasn't a single election in Haiti for four years after Martelly took office; his rule was bloody, authoritarian, and corrupt.[162] When, in August 2015, a vote for parliament was finally allowed, the campaign and balloting were full of violent disruptions, including firefights, several deaths, and vandalized polling stations. The turnout was a risible 15%.[163] A presidential election, held in October 2015, featured 54 candidates for president. Martelly's chosen successor, a previously obscure banana exporter, came in first amid widespread reports of massive fraud; run-off elections were scheduled for December but were postponed until April 2016. Martelly left office in February 2016 without a successor.[164]

On January 12, 2010, Haiti was hammered by a massive earthquake that killed at least 100,000, rendered a quarter-million homeless, and destroyed much of the country's feeble infrastructure. Within days, Barack Obama appointed two of his predecessors, Bill Clinton and George H.W. Bush, as co-czars of the relief effort. On the same day of the appointment, Hillary flew in to meet with President Préval. Four days after the earthquake, she expressed confidence that Haiti would "come back even stronger and better in the future."[165] She said the goal was to "build back better."[166]

From the first, the United States was to be the dominant force in Haiti relief and reconstruction—a point quickly made by the arrival of the 82nd Airborne. The Clintons, one as philanthropist and one as diplomat, were the dominant forces in the U.S. effort. As Jonathan Katz put it in Politico, "The hardest thing about evaluating the Clintons' work in Haiti is that there is so much of it." The Foundation spent scores of millions and raised much more, and the Secretary of State, aside from strong personal involvement, had the embassy and USAID through which to channel help. (Amusingly, both Bill's brother, Roger, and Hillary's brother Hugh tried to work their connections into business deals in Haiti, but only Roger succeeded.)[167] But the enormous effort ended largely in failure. The rubble was cleared, and most people were moved out of refugee camps, but Haiti remains one of the most deeply poor parts of the world. Though there are doubtless some decent things that the Foundation sponsors in Haiti, the overwhelming effect of its interventions lies somewhere between disappointment and disaster.

The U.S. Agency for International Development (USAID), an independent agency that operates under the strategic guidance of the State Department, supervised a lot of the reconstruction efforts.[168] USAID's relief efforts relied heavily on private contractors, who performed poorly despite their high fees. Like any major business sector, the contractors formed a trade association, which hired a PR firm co-founded by the ubiquitous John Podesta.[169]

The marquee project of the Clinton-led reconstruction was the Caracol Industrial Park, which, as Hillary told a roomful of investors at its October 2012 opening, was the sort of thing that would mean "more than providing aid." Rather, it was the kind of investment that "would help the Haitian people achieve their own dreams."[170] It follows a long-standing Clinton model, the public–private partnership of the sort that allows some to do well by doing some kind of good. So far, Caracol has fallen well short of its objectives, producing a mere 6,200 jobs, a tenth of the number promised initially.

The Caracol scheme was also responsible for some dreadful housing. USAID commissioned bids on a plan to build worker housing around Caracol. The scheme was described in an architectural peer review by Greg Higgins as "substandard, inadequate." This was putting it mildly. The houses were tiny, crowded closely together, and lacked running water. They were without flush toilets; occupants would have to make do with a hole in the floor placed right next to the kitchen, which was to be outfitted with little more than a hot plate. The metal roofing proposed for the houses was incapable of standing up to the hurricanes that frequent the region, and could get as hot as 185°F in the summer. Drainage trenches were to run just a few feet from front doors and the sole access to running water for the entire complex was just one half-inch pipe. No provision was made for drainage in an area known to flood.[171] Higgins sent his review to the State Department for investigation, but received little more than a "thank you." According to Higgins, the execution of the plan was as bad as the design—he described the construction as "horrible."[172]

The Clinton Foundation also promised to build "hurricane-proof…emergency shelters that can also serve as schools"—one of which was to be located in the coastal city of

Léogâne. The buildings were to have electricity and plumbing. When *Nation* correspondents Isabel Macdonald and Isabeau Doucet visited the Léogâne site they found the project consisted of "twenty imported prefab trailers beset by a host of problems, from mold to sweltering heat to shoddy construction." The units were made by Clayton Homes, a company owned by the billionaire Warren Buffett, a Foundation member and contributor to Hillary's 2008 campaign whose reputation for decency seems inexplicable. Air samples from the Haitian trailers detected "worrying levels" of the same toxin found in the trailers deployed by FEMA in the wake of Hurricane Katrina, also manufactured by Clayton Holmes. A sixth-grader in one of the trailer schools reported recurring sickening headaches and vision problems. Similar stories came out of the Katrina trailers, but apparently no one at the Clinton Foundation heard them. And Clayton apparently hadn't learned much either: the Haitian trailers were a fresh design, not a simple rehash of the New Orleans models.

The schools never got the plumbing—not even a latrine. According to a wind scientist quoted by Macdonald and Doucet, it seemed unlikely that trailers could be made hurricane-proof, an opinion seconded by a structural engineer who looked at them. When the mayor of Léogâne was told that the Clayton trailers were similar to those provided after Katrina, he said, "It would be humiliating to us, and we'll take this as a black thing."[173]

On another visit to Haiti, in September 2011, Greg Higgins tried to find the trailers, but learned that they'd been removed. The contractor who did the job showed him pictures on his cell phone, but wouldn't say what happened to them.

Clinton interests did, however, succeed in building two new luxury hotels around Port-au-Prince. The Foundation put $2 million of its own money into the Royal Oasis hotel in a suburb of the capital; it's today reported to be largely empty. And Bill was instrumental in getting a Marriott built in the center of the city, introducing its developer—his friend and major donor, the Irish telecoms mogul Denis O'Brien—to Marriott execs. The grand opening in February 2015 featured not only Bill, but Sean Penn as well.[174] Both hotels provided some jobs, of course, but to the many Haitains without housing and short of food, the provision of luxury hotels must have seemed a secondary priority.

In another scheme to accommodate non-Haitians, Hillary's State Department commissioned snazzy housing for the U.S. embassy staff in Port-au-Prince—LEED certified, with a pool and basketball and tennis courts. According to a write-up in the architectural trade press, "The inspiration for the design is derived from the local Haitian culture and is modeled after the

Cubist forms of the 'Bidonvilles' (clustered houses hugging the hillside)."[175] *Bidon* is French for "tin"; reflecting the corrugated metal from which the houses are often made. The term translates as "shanty towns." The design is literally slumming.

The proposed budget was around $100 million for about 100 townhouse units, or about $1 million a unit. Meanwhile, as Higgins pointed out, the budget for building 900 houses for the displaced after the earthquake was around $25 million, about $28,000 a unit. Hillary said that Haiti would be a model for a new kind of economic development, but this doesn't really look like one.[176]

Hillary's people launched a big PR campaign to paint their disastrous Haitian operation as a success, and her emails show that she was very pleased with the results. "A new model of engagement with our own people," she declared, urging her staff to press "Onward!" But as she was writing those celebratory words, daughter Chelsea, on a secret mission to the country, was blunt about the disaster: "the incompetence is mind numbing," she reported. She noted that Haitians were doing a remarkable job of self-organization, with very limited resources—and the outsiders who were supposed to help weren't up to the task. But instead of deferring to the locals—people about whom Bill constantly complained, according to Jonathan Katz—Chelsea urged her father to take even more direct control of the relief efforts: "The Office of Special Envoy—i.e., you Dad—needs authority over the UN and all its myriad parts…"

Of course, Bill and Hillary were already mostly in charge, and their priorities were ass-backward. Katz writes: "The new email tranche shows how quickly the construction of low-wage garment factories and prioritizing exports to the U.S. market came to the center of the U.S.-led response in Haiti." They installed a former Liz Claiborne exec to accelerate the garment strategy.[177] Haitians' needs for food and housing would just have to wait.

POST-STATE

Following her departure from the State Department at the beginning of Obama's second term, Hillary at first sounded like a Bush-era neocon in her criticisms of Obama. In a now notorious interview with Jeffrey Goldberg,[178] she declared her enthusiastic support for Israeli prime minister Benjamin Netanyahu (an unusual position for a Democrat—Democrats usually prefer Labor to Likud in Israel) and for Israel's pummeling of Gaza (not an unusual position for a Democrat). She also made clear that she was against Iran's right to enrich uranium and always had been (though in 2010 she actually said otherwise);[179] and criticized Obama for not having armed the "hard men with the guns" who were fighting against the Assad government in Syria. Some neocons, like Robert Kagan and Max Boot, have recently made supportive noises about Clinton—and with an isolationist tendency rising within the Republican Party, more right-wing advocates of a "muscular" foreign policy might join them as 2016 approaches.[180] Kagan's wife, Victoria Nuland, a former advisor to Dick Cheney, was State Department spokesperson under Clinton. She is most famous for having said "Fuck the EU" in a leaked phone conversation with the U.S. ambassador to Ukraine, because she saw the Europeans as inhibiting a firm anti-Russian stance, which Hillary's confrontation-loving diplomatic team preferred.[181]

Throughout her term as chief diplomat, Hillary seemed perfectly comfortable with calling in airstrikes. She backed an escalation of the Afghanistan war, lobbied on behalf of a continuing military presence in Iraq, urged Obama to bomb Syria, and supported the intervention in Libya. Writing in *Time,* Michael Crowley concluded: "On at least three crucial issues—Afghanistan, Libya, and the bin Laden raid—Clinton took a more aggressive line than [Defense Secretary Robert] Gates, a Bush-appointed Republican."[182]

As the late Richard Holbrooke, who worked in several diplomatic roles for Bill and handled Afghanistan and Pakistan for Hillary at State, said in 2006, "She is probably more assertive and willing to use force than her husband. Hillary Clinton is a classic national-security Democrat."[183] Perhaps this is why none other than Dick Cheney said of her in 2011, "I have a sense that she's one of the more competent members of the current administration and it would be interesting to speculate about how she might perform were she to be president."[184]

A detailed *New York Times* investigation of the run-up to the decision to depose Muammar Qaddafi as ruler of Libya shows her as the crucial force behind the move. Gates described it as a "51–49" decision, and it was Hillary's vigorous support that overcame Obama's ambivalence. (Her top policy aide wrote right before Qaddafi's death that Hillary had "leadership/ownership/stewardship of this country's Libya policy from start to finish.") Hillary does not like ambivalence; her former advisor Anne-Marie Slaughter told the *Times* that when it comes to a choice between action and inaction, she'll choose action. She'd rather be "caught trying." That instinct, plus a deep faith in American power and a belief that her agents in Libya were masters of events, led her to push for the overthrow. It feels eerily like the arrogance and credulousness that produced and prolonged the Vietnam War.[185]

When I interviewed Dick Morris in July 2014, I asked him how he thought Hillary would differentiate herself from Obama in the 2016 campaign. He suggested she'd say that while Obama outlined a beautiful vision, when it came down to it you needed someone who could get things done. And, he added, she'd criticize him for not having armed the Syrian rebels earlier. Two weeks later, Hillary did exactly that. She's nothing if not predictable.

6 PHILANTHROPY INC.

The title of Daniel Halper's book, *Clinton, Inc.*, is key to understanding the family. Unlike the Bush family, neither Bill nor Hillary was born into anything near the ruling class. There was no Prescott Bush—the son of a steel company president who went to Yale, joined Skull and Bones (just like his son and grandson), and later became a banker and then a senator—in their separate pasts. Bill was born poor, in one of the poorest states in the country and into an unstable family, while Hillary was born into the provincial petty bourgeoisie. Entry into elite schools was their ticket to eventual membership in the ruling class; it took decades of striving for them to get there.

Once established, however, politics became the family's business, and it's been very good to them. A 2014 *Wall Street Journal* analysis showed that the Clintons have raised between $2 billion and $3 billion since 1992—more than three-quarters of it from industry sources—for their campaigns, philanthropies, and themselves. At the top of the list of corporate donors were financial firms, and highest up among them was Goldman Sachs. Citigroup and JP Morgan Chase gave generously as well. Not far behind Wall Street were communications/electronics firms and then, that perennial bedrock of Democratic Party support, lawyers and lobbyists. Those three sectors alone contributed more than ten times as much as organized labor, which pitched in just $41 million of the total over the period of the *Journal*'s study.[186]

It's hard to separate the Clintons' personal fortune from the Foundation's; the perks it provides are a form of imputed consumer services, to use the language of national income accounting—jetting all over, staying in fancy hotels, eating very well, and the rest. But they have been prodigious earners on their own account. Bill did most of the heavy financial lifting, earning $105 million from speeches in the dozen years after he left the White House; a good week could yield $1.4 million.[187] According to work by the website 24/7 Wall St, Bill is the 10th-richest of our presidents, with a net worth of $55 million. (Five of the 10 richest presidents have been Democrats, compared to two Republicans, and on average, Democratic presidents are more than three times richer than Republicans.)[188] But Hillary wasn't just sitting around baking cookies: she's worth $32 million, according to a Politico analysis. The property taxes on their two houses, one in D.C. and the other, for which they paid $4.5 million, in Westchester, are

$104,000, twice the average household's income.[189] It's a good life they've made for themselves.

The Foundation's travel expenses alone are striking. According to a 2013 *New York Post* analysis, the Foundation spent over $50 million on air travel over the previous decade—$12 million of it in 2011 alone, "enough to buy 12,000 air tickets costing $1,000 each," or 33 a day.[190] Of course it's true that the Post is a Rupert Murdoch newspaper and might be expected to cast the Clintons in the worst possible light. But before any Democrat says, "Yeah, but that's the Murdoch press!," recall that Rupert threw a fundraiser for Hillary's Senate campaign in 2006 and told *Fortune* that he "could live with" a Hillary presidency.[191] All told, News Corp and other Murdoch properties have given the Clintons over $3 million since 1992, according to a tally by the *Wall Street Journal*, also a Murdoch property.[192]

VALUE FOR MONEY

Wealth porn is always stimulating, but, besides providing the Clintons with a luxurious life, what do all those donations actually mean? According to Donald Trump, it was his contributions that persuaded Hillary to attend his wedding in 2005 (Hillary later claimed she went only because she thought it would be "fun"). But what else have these vast inflows of cash achieved?

On its appearance in May 2015, Peter Schweizer's book *Clinton Cash* was roundly denounced by the Hillary camp, though the more honest members of her intellectual enforcers conceded that its central message—that the family business looks a lot like a lucrative shakedown and influence-peddling operation—did present some image problems. In the *New York Review of Books*, Michael Tomasky worried about a biased media making too much of Schweizer's claims as the presidential campaign began to heat up.[193] It's funny how often the Clinton camp accuses reporters of bias against the Clintons, of an irrational hatred even, as if they'd never done anything to earn the dislike. But Tomasky does recognize that there's a problem:

> A presidency can't have questions like this swirling around it from day one. Imagine speculation that a White House decision with regard to Russia or Pakistan was influenced by a donation to the foundation from someone pursuing a business deal in one of those countries.

After pleading with the Clintons to clean up their act, if only for appearance's sake, Tomasky admits that they probably won't, leading him to a heartstring-tugging final line: "[I]t's hard on a lot of other people."

Apart from his message, Schweizer's résumé gets the Hillary-ites all bent out of shape. He is a conservative who has advised and ghostwritten for Republican politicians. He also appears to have made mistakes in his research, too, some of which were corrected in a revised Kindle edition. And, as the Clintonites like to emphasize, he found no smoking gun—a point that Schweizer himself concedes, more than once:

> The Clintons aren't stupid people. They know the law and take pains to operate within it. Besides, corruption of the kind I have described in this book is very difficult to prove. We cannot ultimately know what goes on in their minds and ultimately prove the links between the money they took in and the benefits that subsequently accrued to themselves, their friends, and their associates. That said, the pattern of behavior I have established is too blatant to ignore, and deserves legal scrutiny by those with investigative capabilities that go beyond journalism.[194]

In other words, a mere journalist can't uncover the smoking gun. You need someone with subpoena power to get to the bottom of it all.

The recurrent pattern of benefits and favors looks too established to be a long series of accidents. I'm not going to quote extensively from Schweizer's book, because it will encourage defenders of Hillary to focus on the source rather than the content. He does, however, make an important point that passed muster with *PolitiFact*: of the thirteen speeches between 2001 and 2012 for which Bill was paid $500,000 or more, ten were given while Hillary was Secretary of State. Many of those speeches were sponsored by groups with interests before the State Department.[195]

Just one other broad point from Schweizer: the prominence of foreign contributors to the Foundation is striking—and the donations are often made by people not known for philanthropy in their home countries. To explain this, Schweizer—accurately—cites an article in the *Indian Express* written by Pratap Bhanu Mehta, not some random internet commenter but a distinguished political scientist, educated at Oxford and Princeton and the president of a New Delhi think tank. Mehta asks a good question, which answers itself: "[T]he top echelons of Indian capital are becoming increasingly global, jockeying for access and influence. What else explains why CII [the Confederation of Indian Industry] was so keen to donate to the Clinton Foundation, when its discharging of its own commitments in India has been, at best, very reluctant?"[196]

Clintonites will also likely decry the *Wall Street Journal* as a fair source of criticism. Nevertheless, its review in early 2015 of what it calls Hillary's "complex corporate ties" is worth attention. It opens by pointing out, as was noted in the previous chapter, that Hillary was unusually aggressive for a Secretary of State at promoting U.S. business abroad, "pushing governments to sign deals and change policies to the advantage of corporate giants such as General Electric Co., Exxon Mobil Corp., Microsoft Corp. and Boeing Co." All these companies gave money to the Clinton Foundation. The Journal counts at least 60 companies that lobbied the State Department during Hillary's reign as having given collectively $26 million to the Foundation. At least 44 of the 60 participated in projects coordinated by the Clinton Global Initiative (CGI).[197]

In *Hard Choices*, Hillary brags about her emphasis on what she calls "economic statecraft," a strategy she concocted with former Goldman Sachs banker Robert Hormats that involves putting the vast U.S. diplomatic corps, with offices in 270 cities around the world, to work "creat[ing] new opportunities for growth and shared prosperity." In the book, this takes the high-minded form of breaking down protectionist barriers and promoting "an open trading system," a core goal of U.S. foreign policy since the end of World War II. The intended beneficiaries are "American companies and workers."[198]

The *Journal* article suggests that less high-minded considerations were involved when theory was turned to practice. In 2009, at the request of Microsoft, Hillary sent Hormats to lobby the Chinese to tighten things up on software piracy. Microsoft, a longtime donor to the Foundation, subsequently launched a CGI-coordinated initiative to provide discounted or free software to teachers and students valued at $130 million. In 2011, Hillary personally lobbied Algeria to buy GE nuclear power equipment; a month after her visit, GE announced a health partnership with the Foundation providing it with between $500,000 and $1 million. (Contributions are reported in ranges, so we don't know exactly how much.) Throughout her tenure, Hillary promoted fracking at home and abroad, a policy supported by major U.S. energy companies, many of whom are also Foundation supporters. Hillary lobbied Russia to buy Boeing planes, rather than those made by Airbus. Soon after, Boeing made its first contribution to the Clinton Foundation. She pressed India to lift restrictions that hampered the growth of Wal-Mart and other U.S.-based big box stores. Hillary, as we have seen, used to lawyer for Wal-Mart and served on its board; the company has given over $1.5 million to the Foundation.

They had it down to a system. Hormats told the *Journal* that before every trip, he provided Hillary with a list of U.S. corporate interests to shill for.

One of the more extravagant stories about the mixing of the mercenary and the eleemosynary in the lives of the Clintons concerns their involvement with the Canadian mining financier Frank Giustra. Although Bill is the leading figure in this drama, Hillary plays an important supporting role.

In September 2005, Giustra flew into Almaty, Kazakhstan, on his private jet. Bill Clinton was aboard. (This wasn't unusual: between 2005 and 2014, Giustra's jet was used for 26 foundation trips, with Giustra and Clinton traveling together for 13 of them. A professional Clinton apologist told me that Bill and his entourage hitched rides on corporate jets because if the Foundation bought its own, the press would hammer them. Better to win favors from moguls.) On arrival, the two were treated to a midnight banquet with the country's president, Nursultan Nazarbayev.

After the dinner, Clinton gave an enthusiastic endorsement for Nazarbayev, who runs a country where dissent is illegal, to lead the Organization for Security and Cooperation in Europe (OSCE), a democracy-promoting, election-watching agency. (Eleven months earlier, Hillary had signed a letter expressing alarm that Kazakhstan might head the group.) Days later, Giustra's company signed an agreement to buy into uranium projects owned by the state-owned uranium agency, Kazatomprom. As the *New York Times* put it, "The monster deal stunned the mining industry, turning an unknown shell company into one of the world's largest uranium producers in a transaction ultimately worth tens of millions of dollars to Mr. Giustra...." Just months later, Giustra donated $31 million to the Clinton Foundation; he's since pledged another $100 million. Both Clinton and Giustra denied there were any connections between these events.

Four months after the Giustra-Clinton visit, Nazarbayev won re-election with 91% of the vote. The OSCE described the election as one featuring "intimidation" and "ballot-box stuffing." Bill nonetheless sent Nazarbayev a congratulatory note expressing the fine sentiment that "Recognizing that your work has received an excellent grade is one of the most important rewards in life."[199]

Five years later, in 2010, Kazakhstan got its OSCE chairmanship—at a time when Hillary was Secretary of State. In her memoir covering this period, Hillary mentions Kazakhstan only three times, all in passing: once as an important military supply line for Afghanistan operations, once in a response to a question on where the former Soviet Central Asian republics fit into U.S. diplomatic plans ("work together on a positive agenda and overcome a long legacy of mistrust"), and once in recounting the awkwardness of an encounter with Silvio Berlusconi at an OSCE summit at a time when his sexual antics were prominently in the news.[200]

There were no words of concern about the awkwardness of attending a democracy and human rights summit in Kazakhstan.

After the Kazakhstan deal, Giustra merged his operations with Uranium One, a South African company that had one of his associates, Ian Telfer, installed as chair. Giustra sold his interest in 2007. Two years later, crisis struck as the head of Kazatomprom was arrested for illegally selling uranium deposits to foreign companies, including Uranium One. There was fear that Uranium One would lose its license. Alarmed, Uranium One pressed the U.S. embassy in Kazakhstan to urge the government to make sure the licenses remained valid. The embassy—under Hillary Clinton's supervision—duly lobbied the government. Several days later, Rosatom, the Russian uranium company, took a 17% stake in Uranium One (one that it would subsequently up to a 51% interest, and later to full control). But to accomplish this, the deal needed U.S. government approval, because Uranium One had U.S. assets (and uranium is no ordinary product).

The agency of the U.S. government that would pass judgment on the deal, the Committee on Foreign Investment in the United States (CFIUS), consists of seven cabinet officers, including the Secretary of State. When a Chinese company tried to buy U.S. uranium deposits in 2009, CFIUS vetoed the deal on national security grounds. Not so the Russian deal; it was approved.

Telfer, the Uranium One chair, gave $2.4 million to the Clinton Foundation between 2009, the year he asked for the embassy's help, and 2012. These contributions were routed through a Canadian foundation that did not appear on the Clinton Foundation's disclosure forms. In addition to these payments, between $1.3 million and $5.6 million was given to the Clinton Foundation with ties to Uranium One. Bill was invited to speak in Moscow for a fee of $500,000—among his bigger paychecks—by Renaissance Capital, a firm with close ties to the Kremlin. Renaissance also gave to a Giustra charity.[201]

Another couple of smelly affairs: UBS and Laureate. First, UBS. The IRS sued the giant Swiss bank to get the identities of Americans with secret accounts and UBS was not pleased. In swept Hillary, in office for just a few weeks, who put together a deal, an unusual activity for a Secretary of State. UBS would turn over information on less than a tenth of the number of accounts the IRS was after. Perhaps by coincidence, UBS's contributions to the Clinton Foundation rose tenfold over the next few years and the bank paid Bill Clinton $1.5 million to participate in a few Q&A sessions with their top wealth manager.[202]

And second, Laureate. Hillary is now critical of for-profit universities, proposing tougher regulation, though not the closure of this smelly line of business, which is what it deserves. Its business model depends largely on government loans to students, who pay rich tuitions for often-worthless degrees.[203] While Secretary of State, however, she urged that Laureate Education, a global for-profit college operation noted for bringing U.S.-style huckstering to the outside world, be included at a State Department dinner on education policy. She described it in a 2009 email as "the fastest growing college network in the world…started by Doug Becker who Bill likes a lot. It's a for-profit model that should be represented." Soon after that email was written, Laureate, backed by investors like Henry Kravis (a Republican) and George Soros (a Democrat), hired Bill Clinton as its honorary chairman, a position he resigned from in early 2015 as Hillary's campaign began.[204] The role brought him $16.5 million. Bill also took in over $2 million from GEMS Education, a Dubai-based company that runs preschool and K–12 programs. (That was, as *Bloomberg Politics* points out, part of the $139 million they made over the eight years ending in 2014, putting them securely in the top 0.01%.)[205]

In Latin America, Laureate appears to run some decent institutions, but others are, as the *Washington Post* put it, run by "turbocharging enrollment, often without a parallel increase in academic investment." In the words of a Brazilian legislator who led an investigation of Laureate, "they have turned education into a commodity that focuses more on profit than knowledge." The business plan is driven by low admissions standards, marketing, cost-cutting, and student debt. Becker, the one Bill likes a lot (but who never went to college himself), defends his operation by saying, "The choice was to be highly ranked or have a viable scale."[206] Bill and Hillary, of course, went to Georgetown, Wellesley, Oxford, and Yale.

Life can be full of strange coincidences, no doubt. Perhaps Hillary had no knowledge of any apparent quid pro quos. These transactions—the official work done on behalf of private interests, the generous contribution of those private interests to a vast family philanthropic enterprise—may turn out to have been entirely legal. No one without subpoena power can know for sure. But the deals, like the Clinton family itself, are beautiful emblems of our system of political economy at its highest level: the intimate bonding of public and private through money.

Contributions aside, the sight of our top diplomat so baldly playing the huckster for the Fortune 500 puts one in mind of this passage from *The Communist Manifesto*: "The bourgeoisie has stripped of its halo every occupation hitherto honored and looked up to with reverent awe." Not to over-idealize diplomats, of course.

PHILANTHROPIC WORK

Clinton fans counter all this smelly stuff by arguing that the Foundation does good work, pointing with special pride to its initiatives on AIDS in Africa. It's indisputable that some good has come about as result of the Foundation's projects, but overall, its impact points to profound structural limitations of the philanthropic approach to social problems—a strategy promoted by the neoliberal stripping of the state of its better functions and passing off the business of melioration to foundation program officers.

According to the audited financial statements of the Clinton Health Access Initiative (CHAI)—the part of the many-armed enterprise that carries out AIDS work—total program expenses in 2013 (the most recent year available) were $99 million, up from $69 million the previous year.[207] Of the total 2013 program spending, almost $31 million went to salaries, and just $2 million for procurement (less than for office expenses). CHAI's net assets increased by 42% between 2012 and 2013, to $36 million; it's not clear why an entity focused on improving the health of the very poor needs such a large stash of assets relative to expenses.

The financial statements don't break out spending by disease; programs to address tuberculosis, malaria, and other maladies are included in the total. According to CHAI's tax return, the enterprise spent just short of $30 million on AIDS.[208] If the AIDS "procurement" expenditures are similar to their overall share of the Initiative's overall spending, something like $600,000 was devoted to purchasing supplies.

The small sums spent on procurement reflect the Initiative's emphasis on negotiating lower drug prices rather than providing the drugs themselves. In a note included in the financial statements, it claims to have "helped more than 8.2 million people in 70 countries" since its founding in 2002, generating $1 billion in savings between 2011 and 2015 alone. Just how these people were "helped" and how they were counted is not disclosed.

CHAI also engages in classically Clintonesque micro-initiatives, like improving supply chains, facilitating bulk purchases, and identifying "high-impact interventions."[209] It's all reminiscent of Bill's budget documents, where the prose was full of grand statements about investing in people, but the sums were barely visible when you scrutinized the numbers: $100 million overall, and $30 million on AIDS, is not a lot of money.

Contrast this with Clinton's successor, the deservedly maligned George W. Bush, who nonetheless made a large U.S. government commitment to fighting AIDS in poor countries, mainly in Africa. The President's Emergency Plan for AIDS Relief (PEPFAR) was begun in 2003 with $15 billion in funding for the next three years (which Congress subsequently raised to $18.8 billion). It brought antiretroviral therapy to 2 million with HIV and provided care to 10 million. Between 2004 and 2008, it supported prevention of mother-to-child HIV transmission in nearly 16 million pregnancies.[210] In 2008, the program was granted another $39 billion, with a goal of treating at least 3 million, caring for

12 million, and preventing 12 million new infections.[211] Surprisingly, perhaps, Barack Obama has cut PEPFAR funding significantly—even though his first Secretary of State (Hillary, in other words) publicly declared that achieving an AIDS-free generation was a "policy priority."[212]

CHAI may do good work, but there's just no comparison between what a philanthropy can do and what a well-organized, well-funded public program—with on the order of 60 times CHAI's funding—is able to achieve. Bush's PEPFAR saved millions of lives; CHAI cannot make anything remotely like that claim.

THE NEXT GENERATION

Bill and Hillary are looking to institutionalize the work of the Foundation so it lasts beyond them. They're aiming to raise a $250 million endowment.[213] And they look to be grooming daughter Chelsea to inherit the family business.

Chelsea Clinton has come a long way from when journalist/provocateur Tom Gogola imagined her as the White House riot grrrl:

> Let's inhale
> let's go to jail

let's call Janet Reno
when we need to make bail
Let's inhale
till we're meltin'
do vodka shots
with comrade Yeltsin[214]

Chelsea was, in reality, doing none of those things. Instead, she was going to Sidwell Friends School, the posh, progressive private school in D.C., and then on to Stanford (B.A., history), Oxford (M.Phil., international relations), and Columbia (Masters in Public Health). She's never had much trouble getting work. Most famous was her short career as a TV newsperson, during which she did next to nothing for a $600,000 salary.[215] Barry Diller, presumably impressed by her keen business acumen after somewhat less brief stints with a hedge fund and McKinsey, appointed her to the board of his company, IAC, which is good for a $50,000 annual retainer and a $250,000 stock grant at the age of 31.[216]

Chelsea is also joining her parents by getting into the speaking racket. When the University of Missouri at Kansas City recoiled at Hillary's speaking fee of $275,000, they did the next best thing and booked Chelsea for a mere $65,000—well above Gloria Steinem's $30,000 standard, and Tina Brown's $50,000, and those are two people who might potentially have interesting things to say. Chelsea's stipulations were classic *Clinton, Inc.* marketing materials, opening remarks, and the guest list would have to be Foundation-approved; she would be required to speak for just 10 minutes, endure a 20-minute, moderated Q&A session, and would then spend 30 minutes posing for pics with local VIPs. Though the event she spoke at was a fundraiser, the university appears to have raised almost $30,000 less than her fee.[217]

Chelsea's wedding to hedge-funder Marc Mezvinsky was one of the social highlights of 2010. (Mezvinsky's social pedigree is not quite as sterling as his bride's: his father did time in federal prison for fraud—crimes he committed in part to recover the funds he'd lost to Nigerian email scams.) The nuptials, held on a 50-acre spread overlooking the Hudson, featured $15,000 worth of top-of-the-line Port-A-Potties and $600,000 for air-conditioned tents. The total bill is estimated at $3 to 5 million.[218]

Chelsea is now fully assimilated into the family business, with a personal staff almost as big as her father's and with her mother's habit of alienating colleagues.[219] She has her work cut out for her. The Foundation's reputation has been tarnished by revelations about the scope and sources of its funding and the aura of quid pro quo around it. According to *Politico*, donors and celebs have become "wary" of the enterprise, and it experienced an unusually large number of refusals of invitations to its annual extravaganza in September 2015. Membership renewals are down. Among the dropouts: Samsung, Exxon Mobil, HSBC, and DeutscheBank. Goldman Sachs, however, remains loyal.

Chelsea appears to be part of the problem. As *Politico* put it, "sources who have recruited participants for CGI say it's become increasingly difficult to raise money from large companies for meetings in which executives would just as likely appear on panels with Chelsea Clinton, rather than one of her parents." Things have gotten so rough that Arianna Huffington, a past headliner, turned down an invitation, opting to spend her time instead at a "thought leaders" conference hosted by Charlie Rose.[220]

If her mother doesn't win in November 2016, it might be time for Chelsea to enter politics, lest the family connections go cold.

7 TOWARD NOVEMBER 2016

Hillary commenced the 2016 campaign season in the style she entered the 2008 affair: as the "inevitable front-runner." Early on, she embarked on the project of re-introducing herself to us, something she's done several times before during her four decades in politics—after the health care flop, with her first Senate campaign, with her failed first presidential campaign. And it was said of this re-re-reintroduction, as was said before, that her challenge would be to appear more warm and spontaneous, which is difficult for someone who, in public at least, is obviously neither. Unlike her husband, who has a roving mind, vast interests, and an enthusiasm that comes across in public, Hillary has a mind that tends toward the procedural. As Dick Morris put it, she's like "a trial lawyer who fights for a position, but she's not creative and she's not a broad strategic policy thinker."[221] Bill is, and their skills are powerfully complementary; neither would have gotten this far alone.

Hillary's personality makes for a stiff candidate. Unlike her husband, she's not a natural with crowds—her awkwardness at connecting with people makes her prone to gaffes like claiming they were "dead broke" on leaving the White House. She's long been paranoid about the press, which is not the best way to get indulgent coverage. A longtime associate of both hers and Bill's relayed their opinion of reporters to Carl Bernstein: "Her ground zero assumption is that you're an asshole. His ground zero assumption is that you're an asshole, but he can charm you."[222] At a July 2015 appearance in a small town in New Hampshire, her aides kept the horde of reporters walking ahead of her, separated from the candidate by a rope. Reporters ran backward, asking questions that she tried not to answer, as a right-wing heckler trailed her from the rear.[223] That arrangement was emblematic of the difficulties that struck her campaign the moment it left the realm of the notional and hit the road.

In her latest reinvention, Hillary tried to appropriate some of Brooklyn's current cool by locating her campaign headquarters there. But instead of going for a new media hotbed like (gentrified) Williamsburg or the artier (gentrifying) Bushwick, she instead chose Brooklyn Heights—often called "America's first suburb"—one of the richest, whitest neighborhoods in all of New York City. She shot a short video celebrating her arrival in Brooklyn that featured mostly well-heeled residents of the neighborhood enjoying its posh infrastructure. The homogenous cast of the Brooklyn video contrasted sharply with her announcement video's studied diversity, shot somewhere out in the Real America, in which she pledged to work on behalf of "everyday Americans."[224] That term is said to be a replacement for the more traditional "middle class" in a society where fewer people feel like they're part of the middle class.[225] ("Working class" would be a touchier term, both for Hillary, who knows that whatever she is it's certainly not a member of the proletariat, and the broad swathes of working Americans, who don't always like to be reminded of their status.)

Hillary's standing as a front-runner eroded with remarkable speed. A host of critical stories appeared, ranging, as we've seen earlier, from what looked like influence peddling around the family foundations to the email affair. True to their reflex, Clinton partisans blamed an irrationally hostile media. But the revelations chipped away at her standing in the polls, causing her to lose ground even among Democratic women.

The much-touted but never-announced challenge from Massachusetts senator Elizabeth Warren evaporated, momentarily solidifying Hillary's standing. Though Warren is famous for her anti-bankster provocations, her politics otherwise have never been terribly progressive. On foreign affairs, a topic that doesn't seem to hold much interest for Warren (a *Boston Globe* investigation found that she was one of only four senators who hadn't taken an official trip abroad as of August 2014), the evidence is that she is little different from Hillary.[226] She scurried away from questions about the Middle East when confronted by a reporter from a conservative website in a hotel lobby.[227] Glenn Greenwald characterized her defense of Israel's bombing of Gaza as essentially indistinguishable from Clinton's—or Netanyahu's.[228] Those who wanted Warren to run were drawn to her anti–Wall Street agitation—her support of tighter regulation and breaking up the megabanks—positions that Hillary tried to shadow, unconvincingly.

And then a real challenge emerged from an unexpected quarter: Vermont senator Bernie Sanders, a self-described democratic socialist from a tiny state with neither big money nor organization behind him. From a genuinely progressive perspective, Sanders too has significant shortcomings in his foreign policy positions, especially in relation to Israel. He was supportive of Israel's vicious 2014 assault on Gaza. But he did oppose the Iraq War and seems committed to a full withdrawal from Afghanistan. And on domestic issues, and especially those relating to inequality, he has spoken more forcefully than Warren and certainly more consistently and credibly than Clinton, whose newfound commitment to a more egalitarian America and vigorous control of Wall Street sits uneasily with acceptance of $400,000 for a couple of speeches to Goldman Sachs in 2013.[229] Though Sanders is not a socialist in the stricter senses of the word, his domestic politics are cut from the cloth of traditional social democracy, which makes him a virtual Bolshevik by modern American standards.

After Warren's attacks softened up Hillary on the issue of regulation of Wall Street, forcing her to channel a very mild dose of the 19th-century populist William Jennings Bryan, Sanders attacked on the inequality front, forcing her, together with a chorus of supporters at outlets like *Salon* and *The Nation*, to make highly ludicrous claims about her long-standing populism. *Salon* headed a June 2015 piece by Heather "Digby" Parton with: "Hillary shocker: Who needs Elizabeth Warren? Clinton unleashes inner liberal, media freaks out."[230] (Sanders was still chopped liver in this universe.) *Slate* expressed surprise that Hillary had moved "so far and so fast to the left."[231] The credulous reaction to Hillary's heavily focus-grouped "left turn" in the early days of the primary campaign is further proof that Democrats, especially liberal Democrats, are the cheapest dates around—throw them a few rhetorical bones, regardless of your record, and they're yours to take home and bed.

Alongside acclaiming the "left-turn," Hillaryites busied themselves with wheeling out the tropes of vulgar identity politics to defend their candidate. First out of the gate was Dara Lind in *Vox*.[232] In a maneuver that would become standard for the genre, Lind began by acknowledging Bernie's appeal: "there are a lot of those progressives out there who are very concerned about economic inequality, the rise of the super-rich, the financial industry,

and the role of money in American politics." But the focus on economic issues slights the concerns of "other progressives—many of
them black or Latino" about biased policing, mass incarceration,
and maltreatment of immigrants. (Actually, polling data show
that blacks and Latinos care a lot about economic issues—no surprise, given their increased risk of poverty and unemployment
compared to whites.)[233] Lind points to Hillary Clinton as "the
Democratic candidate who's spoken out the most about the concerns that animate nonwhite progressives." Lind doesn't mention
that Hillary supported Bill's 1994 crime bill, cheering the legion
of new cops it helped fund and greasing the incarceration boom
that she now says she's against.[234] Nor does she mention Hillary's
support of Bill's "end of welfare as we know it," which hit black
and Latino women hard. Days later, *Salon*'s Joan Walsh, who once
confessed that she too was "behind much of Bill Clinton's 1996
welfare reform," weighed in, reproducing Lind's argument and
tweaking Sanders and Warren over their refusal to embrace the
Black Lives Matter movement—though there could be little doubt
that the redistributionist policies that Sanders advocates would do
far more material good for black Americans than anything Hillary
is likely to promote (in deed, not word).[235] Anticipating such ar-
guments, Walsh insisted that redistribution would still fail to address "the core issue of criminal justice reform." (Most people in
prison were quite poor before they got there, but apparently that's

not part of the core "core.") And who is addressing these issues? Why, Hillary, of course. "The woman who stumbled facing Barack Obama" may be the "unlikely beneficiary of white progressives' stumbles on race."

Criticism of Sanders for initially being less than forthright and passionate about mass incarceration and the plague of killer cops was certainly justified. These are among the worst features of contemporary American life and it is to be cheered that as the summer of 2015 passed, Sanders addressed more attention to them. But if there is substance to the Lind/Walsh critique of Sanders, it can hardly be used to flatter Hillary. As law professor Douglas Berman wrote on his blog, during the 2008 campaign, Hillary criticized Obama for his stance against mandatory minimum sentences (a stance that Obama seemed to forget on taking office) and took a position "to the right of Justice Scalia on sentencing issues."[236] Hillary's new line puts one in mind of T.S. Eliot's assessment of the poet John Donne: "About Donne there hangs the shadow of the impure motive; and impure motives lend their aid to a facile success."

Soon after the appearance of Walsh's *Salon* piece, *The Nation* published a political psychoanalysis by dial-a-quote law professor Stephen Gillers that dismissed concerns about Clinton family ethics as grossly overblown. "Let's stipulate that Hillary Clinton will always put the public first and that she knows she will. What she has to figure out is how to make sure the public believes it, too," Gillers asseverated, paying little heed to the notion that, in law at least, stipulation is something that two parties have to agree to, rather than one simply uttering it *ex cathedra*. He attributed "criticism of Hillary's ethics" to anxieties around "the rise of women in politician and professional life. A lot of people still have a problem with powerful women."[237] It seemed not to occur to Gillers that one could have issues with how a woman uses that power.

In another ingenious stroke, Rebecca Traister—author of a 2008 book about Hillary, or more precisely the conflicted appeal of Hillary to her demographic—took to *The New Republic* to argue that the New Hillary is actually a return to the Old Hillary, the rambunctious feminist and social uplifter, who was kept under wraps for two or three decades during her husband's time in the limelight.[238] True to Hillary's old, now-recovered self, Hillary's official campaign kickoff was held on Roosevelt Island (just offshore from Manhattan), which, according to Traister, was intended to signify the return of the Democratic Party from its neoliberal detour to its FDR roots. A more skeptical interpretation of the locale selected might be that access to Roosevelt Island is, from a security point of view, easy to manage. Hillary and her people like to be in control of events.

In October, writing in *Elle*, Traister upped the ante, accusing anyone who didn't support Hillary of sexism and characterizing Hillary's critics as "liberal" and her defense of her as "radical." This trope, which is widely employed, makes Hillary the representative of all women, so that attacks on her become attacks on "us." This is desperation seeking to operate as political blackmail.[239] If you don't like Hillary, you just don't like women.

This sort of privileging of gender at any cost found some exuberant support across the Atlantic when the British Labour Party elected the socialist Jeremy Corbyn as its leader in September 2015. A phalanx of neoliberal feminists uncorked denunciations of Corbyn and his comrades as "brocialists," indifferent to the needs of women. Daisy Benson's intervention in *The Independent* was characteristic, concluding with the assertion that "the only truly progressive thing for Labour to do would be to elect a female leader this time around—no matter what her policies are."[240] If only Walsh and Lind could be that blunt. Traister is getting there.

The contorted apologetics reached peak absurdity with an intervention by Anthony Weiner, the former New York Congressman who was disgraced in a sexting scandal. Weiner questioned Bernie Sanders' party loyalty in opposing Hillary. This sat oddly with the fact that Sanders, though running in the Democratic primary, had never previously identified as a Democrat. Despite the criticism, Weiner acknowledges that Bernie is his "kind of politician," who "always got [him] fired up to make the fighting wing of the Democratic Party feistier," and whose "battle cry on behalf of working Americans is almost as good as Hillary Clinton's."[241]

In the context of these improbable claims, Weiner was required to disclose that his wife "works for Hillary." In fact, Huma Abedin, whom we met earlier as a State Department special employee, started working for Hillary in 1996 and has been in her employ in a variety of capacities pretty much ever since. They are so close that Hillary said at a pre-wedding celebration for the couple that if she "had a second daughter, it would [be] Huma."

When they're not funny, there's something odd about these defenses of Hillary, which cheer on the part of her that's running against many of the policies that she and her husband previously embraced. Of course people can change their minds, and it's sometimes admirable when they do. But in Hillary's case, political calculation generally appears to trump genuine shifts in conviction. The left turn seems primarily to derive from her understanding of the mistakes that she made in her 2008 campaign against Obama. Then, she resolutely hewed to the center, which is not what Democratic primary voters wanted after Bush, war, and economic crisis. In 2015, by contrast, she presented herself as always the friend of "everyday Americans" while admitting that her vote for the war, which she previously defended, had been a "mistake."

But for all this change of focus, by one critical test the "talk left" strategy that Hillary employed in the early stages of the primary campaign simply didn't work: she has continued to experience trouble raising money from small and medium donors—the kinds of people who can form a critical activist base for her campaign.[242] Even mainstream Democrats like former Pennsylvania governor Ed Rendell conceded that Bernie enthusiasm was doing her damage among the activist base.

The third-quarter 2015 fundraising numbers were surprising: Hillary raised $28 million, taking her total to $75 million for the year. But that was down about a third from the previous quarter, and not all that far ahead of Sanders' $25 million, which took his total for the year to $40 million. And Sanders had collected a million donations from 650,000 different donors by October 1, milestones that Obama didn't reach until February 2008.[243] Sanders' fundraising in early 2016 continued strong; he raised over $40 million in February, double his January total, and again overwhelmingly from small donors.[244] Bernie is almost certain to fade and Hillary to prevail, but these numbers suggest that the public mood is more amenable to a serious appeal from the left than it has been for decades.

Hillary's team seemed especially desperate for small donors as various reporting deadlines loomed, sending out multiple emails begging for as little as a dollar to show how many people were "part of this organization." She needs the financiers' money badly, but she also needs the smaller contributions to look like something other than a tool of the oligarchy.

Of course, she was working the high end too. In late September 2015, Hillary hit check-bearing parties in and around New York, including one hosted by financier Cliff Robbins, the model for the book and movie *Barbarians at the Gate*.[245] But even the high end isn't without problems. Some of the oligarchs backing the campaign were beginning to look nervous about the caliber of people turning out for fundraising events. An early fall money-chasing tour of L.A. included occasions sponsored by "the absolute B team," one check bundler told the *Los Angeles Times*.[246] A review of her "bundlers"—people who gather contributions from their network of rich friends—by *USA Today* found a large number of Obama bundlers missing.[247]

To some degree Hillary has been able to compensate for these shortfalls by a more rigorous control of expenses, certainly more rigorous than she managed in her 2008 run. Then, early on in the campaign, she burned through money while her advisors fought with each other, sometimes publicly, badly undermining her claims to be the seasoned manager. In 2015 she ran a much tighter ship, so much so that her campaign was widely staffed with unpaid interns who were told to take the $14 Bolt

Bus between New York and D.C. and to use their own cell phones to make business calls.[248]

Money aside, it was clear that Hillary was not creating anything like the buzz of the senator from Vermont running to her left. With no advertising and only a minimal professional media operation (supplemented by almost 200,000 volunteers, mostly online), Sanders was attracting huge crowds across the country—15,000 in Seattle, 20,000 in Boston, 27,000 in Los Angeles, 28,000 in Portland. Meanwhile Hillary was doing well to draw 5,000.[249] Sanders even got a sizable audience at Liberty University, the fundamentalist institution founded by Jerry Falwell, where Sanders urged those attending to take the Bible's words about peace and aiding the poor seriously. Clinton's staff, in contrast, were forced to close off floor space in large venues to make the meager crowds look more dense than they were.[250]

EMAIL SCANDAL BLOWS

Despite Bernie Sanders' claim in the debate broadcast by CNN on October 13, 2015 that the issue was of little concern to most Americans, Hillary's decision to use a private email server while Secretary of State has caused her 2016 campaign lots of trouble. She seems unable to understand why these scandals befall her, though. From her complaints about the "vast right-wing conspiracy" in the 1990s—which was real, for sure, but had plenty of raw material to work with—to her initial dismissal of the email scandal as merely "political," Hillary evidently believes that people just have it in for her. Her use of "political" as a term of dismissal is curious for someone who's spent almost her entire professional life in and around politics.

For weeks Hillary treated the email scandal as something of a joke. In that great presidential tradition of George W. Bush yukking it up about WMDs and Barack Obama milking drone strikes for their comic potential, Hillary said to the Iowa Democratic Wing Ding in August 2015: "You may have seen that I recently launched a Snapchat account. I love it. I love it. Those messages disappear all by themselves." [251] Only a few days later, when asked at a news conference whether she had "wiped" her email server, she answered: "I don't know, I have no idea. Like with a cloth or something?"[252] But apparently she didn't wipe it, or have it wiped, leaving the real possibility that the deleted emails could be recovered.[253]

As summer turned to fall, Hillary's poll numbers kept dropping, and the email scandal, which fueled doubts about her trustworthiness, was one of the prime reasons. But her partisans would hear none of it. To them, the scandal was a Republican plot abetted by a hostile press. The most extravagant media criticism from Camp Clinton comes from family attack dog David Brock, who has a particular beef with the *New York Times*, which he describes as a "megaphone for conservative propaganda"—a description that would surprise actual conservatives—deserving of "a special place in hell."[254] It's as if Hillary had never done anything to warrant scrutiny—or as if penning reporters behind rope is the way to encourage friendlier coverage.

The less loyal disagree. Hillary's use of a private server looks perfectly symptomatic of her desire for secrecy and control. It's reminiscent of the lockdown under which her health care scheming was conducted and the treatment of the Whitewater billing records. Could the deleted emails contain some trading of diplomatic favors for contributions to the Foundation? Might they contain state secrets, improperly communicated? We may never find out, but to normal people, those not intoxicated by the Clinton charm, it all looks shady.

Hillary did, finally, give up joking about the emails and apologize directly—but not before offering a characteristic pseudo-apology: "I disagree with the choice that I made. At the end of the day, I am sorry that this has been confusing to people."[255] (At least she didn't say "I am not a crook.") A few days later, though, she wrote in a mass email, "Yes, I should have used two email addresses, one for personal matters and one for my work at the State Department. Not doing so was a mistake. I'm sorry about it, and I take full responsibility." She decided to write the email after watching the deliberations of a focus group.[256]

BLM

A month or two after Walsh, Lind, et al. launched their attacks on Sanders, a handful of Black Lives Matter (BLM) activists disrupted appearances by him and (the largely overlooked) Martin O'Malley at the Netroots Nation conference, and by Sanders alone at a rally in defense of Social Security and Medicare in Seattle. Both candidates were criticized for failing to come up with a criminal justice reform agenda, and for not explicitly addressing the racism involved in America's intense police violence and mass incarceration.

O'Malley quickly put out a criminal justice platform. It had some good stuff in it, but shied away from a condemnation of America's national habit of over-criminalizing and over-policing in general. Though some activists seemed placated, O'Malley has a lot to answer for.[257] In 2005, while he was Mayor of Baltimore, he ran an uncompromising "zero tolerance" policy that led to over 100,000 arrests in a city of 600,000. The former head of the city's NAACP chapter, Marvin Cheatham, said, "Martin did damage to us." And city councilman Brandon Scott, who was harassed by cops as a teenager, insisted that zero-tolerance was "one of the major aspects of the breakdown of Baltimore."[258]

Sanders' initial reaction to the BLM disruption looked awkward, and he was slower than O'Malley to respond. His staff did offer to meet with both the Seattle disruptors and the founders of BLM, but both invitations were rejected.[259] As someone posting on Twitter as Dr. Cornel Fresh put it: "Why shut down those sanders rallies with no ask? Then when sanders folks try to rap with you it's 'nah.'"[260]

Sanders also invited celebrity activist DeRay Mckesson in for a meeting. That prompted some grumbling from BLM activists who resented Mckesson's self-appointed leadership status—understandable, because by some accounts Mckesson performs largely for the media, but also confusing, since it's not clear who is an authentic spokesperson for an organization that, despite having a board and offering franchises to local chapters, presents itself as decentered and leaderless.

Mckesson is hardly a full-spectrum rebel. He has a long history with Teach for America (TFA), a neoliberal project to break teachers' unions and displace long-tenured teachers (disproportionately black), replacing them with fresh (disproportionately white) graduates of elite schools. (Mckesson is a Bowdoin grad.) These posh temps work 60- or 70-hour weeks for a couple of years before moving on to law school or

Goldman Sachs. Mckesson has cheered on charter schools—a concerted attack on public education, popular with hedge fund managers—on Twitter. Apparently inspired by his experience with TFA, Mckesson declared on Twitter that an op-ed recommending the privatization of the post office was an "interesting read."

Mckesson would fit well into the Obama-Clinton Democratic Party. He may be happy to join; as he tweeted in October, "In the movement space, I've seen people just attach 'capitalism' and 'neoliberalism' to everything they disagree with. It's fascinating."[261] The use of corporate language like "movement space" is strange coming from someone who identifies as a "protester."

The Boston branch of BLM's meeting with Hillary provided its own drama. After the announcement of plans via *The New Republic*'s Jamil Smith to disrupt one of her press conferences in New Hampshire, the Secret Service closed the event. Several BLM representatives met privately with Hillary and a video of the proceedings was released to the public. What was most remarkable about the meeting is how the activists seemed more interested in what was in Hillary's heart, and the feelings of white people generally, rather than in actual policy changes. Hillary's response was sharp:

[Y]ou're going to have to come together as a movement

and say, "Here's what we want done about it." Because you can get lip service from as many white people as you can pack into Yankee Stadium and a million more like it, who are going to say, "Oh, we get it. We get it. We're going to be nicer..." I don't believe you change hearts. I believe you change laws, you change allocation of resources, you change the way systems operate. You're not going to change every heart. You're not.... You can keep the movement going, which you have started, and through it you may actually change some hearts. But if that's all that happens, we'll be back here in 10 years having the same conversation.[262]

It's hard for me to write, but this is a rare occasion where Hillary is absolutely right. While it's certainly important to point out that her political history of support for her husband's awful crime and welfare bills makes her current stance against mass incarceration and police violence suspect, BLM activists seem reluctant to make specific demands. (In October, what is presumably the "official" BLM website put out a set of guiding principles that sounded separatist and a little New Age-y, without a word, as the young writer R.L. Stephens pointed out, about the working-class black men who are the disproportionate victims of the criminal justice system.)[263] It's all very reminiscent of Occupy, this emphasis on a decentered non-structure and a hesitance about embracing an agenda. But Hillary understands how power works, even if she's systematically on the wrong side of it.

A few weeks after the meeting, the Democratic National Committee officially endorsed BLM, whatever that means precisely—and BLM rejected the endorsement with a statement posted to Facebook:

> More specifically, the Black Lives Matter Network is clear that a resolution from the Democratic National Committee won't bring the changes we seek. Resolutions without concrete change are just business as usual. Promises are not policies. We demand freedom for Black bodies, justice for Black lives, safety for Black communities, and rights for Black people. We demand action, not words, from those who purport to stand with us.
>
> While the Black Lives Matter Network applauds political change towards making the world safer for Black life, our only endorsement goes to the protest movement we've built together with Black people nationwide—not the self-interested candidates, parties, or political machine seeking our vote.[264]

While it's perfectly understandable that the activists don't want to be co-opted or hijacked by a bunch of opportunists, it's not clear what political strategy lies behind this rejection. If you spend a month or two harassing and lobbying Democratic presidential candidates and then reject their endorsement, rather than treating it as a pledge you intend to hold them to, what is your vision of social change, and what understanding of power is it based on? It's hard to escape the feeling that BLM is characteristic of so much dissent today: more about self-affirmation and healing than about taking power.

To be effective, any reversal of the incarceration boom and police violence will have to be part of a broad agenda of reform. As Touré Reed wrote in an article on the long history of liberals' separating of race and class, "in the 1930s and 1940s mainstream African-American civil rights leaders…frequently argued that precisely because most blacks were working class, racial equality could only be achieved through a combination of anti-discrimination policies and social-democratic economic policies." But with the purges of the Cold War, this perspective disappeared.[265]

And, as Leah Gordon argued in *From Power to Prejudice*, philanthropists have long been steering social science research on race away from systemic studies of power to psychologized analyses of individual attitudes.[266] The BLM analysis of race relations emphasizes the psychological wage that whites earn from their alleged superiority, an explanation that has a lot in common with liberal tendencies to psychologize power—the white cop's bloodlust, say, in shooting an unarmed black man rather than the complex systems of hierarchy and exploitation that put both of them into confrontation.

While blacks are far more likely to be imprisoned or shot by cops than whites, almost twice as many white people are killed by cops as blacks, and the white incarceration rate is, in itself, a global disgrace. Any political movement to change U.S. criminal justice policy needs a broad demographic base to make a difference.

According to the *Washington Post's* count, of the 748 people shot dead by cops in the first nine months of 2015, almost half, 363, were white; a quarter, or 189, were black, and 121, Hispanic/Latino.[267] Relative to population, blacks are about two-and-a-half times more likely to get killed by a cop than are whites; Latinos, only slightly more likely than whites. British cops shoot dead on average two people a year; Australians, four or five; Germans, seven or eight.[268] American cops blow away almost three people every day. As atrocious as the black figures are—and they are absolutely horrible—the white death rate alone, based on international comparisons, is in a class by itself.

The disproportionality of imprisonment is far greater. A white man has a 1 in 17 chance of going to prison; a Latino man, 1 in 6; a black man, 1 in 3. (The rates for women are about one-sixth the rate for men in the same demographic.) The Latino and black numbers are so extreme that you can fail to notice that the white one is still a form of madness. In 2013, 478 of every 100,000 white men were in prison, 1,134 of every 100,000 Latino men, and 2,805 of every 100,000 black men. Again, the last two numbers are so mindboggling that you might forget that just 79 per 100,000 Germans are incarcerated.[269] In France, it's 91 per 100,000 overall—and 582 for noncitizens of North African origin, less than the rate for whites in Florida.[270]

American society has a deep punitive streak that's nearly unrivaled in the world. It catches an enormous number of people in its net—especially the poor and marginalized, a demographic that the United States produces in huge quantities. Reversing mass incarceration and ending police violence are urgent tasks if we ever want to resemble a civilized society, but framing it in purely racial terms misses the breadth of state violence and reduces the constituency for change.

And little of it can change without a serious redistributionist agenda—undoing the vast, heavily racialized disparities in income and wealth in the United States, the persistent (and heavily racialized) educational and residential segregation, and the predilection to manage (heavily racialized) social conflict with cops, courts, and prisons. Regardless of what she says at a campaign event, Hillary can contribute almost nothing to that necessary transformation.

REDBAITING BERNIE

The Sanders campaign forced Hillary and other mainstream Democrats to reveal themselves as the corporate tools they've always been. She, her surrogates, and her court intellectuals have become the party of the finger-wagging "No!" Hillary rejected Sanders' free college tuition proposals, saying "everybody has to have some skin in this game." She's denounced him as a budget-buster who'd increase the size of government by 40%. Rep. John Lewis, almost always described with the epithet "civil rights icon," rejected Sanders' proposal for tuition-free public universities by thundering: "There's not anything free in America. We all have to pay for something.... I think it's very misleading to say to the American people, we're going to give you something free."[271]

Actually, the University of California and the City University of New York were free until the 1970s—CUNY was established as a free university in an 1847 referendum—but the crackdown of the 1970s required the imposition of tuition at these institutions.

As Roger Freeman, an educational advisor to Richard Nixon and Ronald Reagan, put it in 1970, "We are in danger of producing an educated proletariat. That's dynamite! We have to be selective on who we allow to go through higher education." Students need some "skin in the game," and if they have no skin to spare, tough on them.

H. Bruce Franklin quotes Freeman's outburst in an excellent short essay on the turn from something of a welfare state to the carceral state in the 1970s. As Franklin argues, the shift in spending priorities from free—or, in other jurisdictions, low-cost—college to mass incarceration was part of an intensification of social discipline: people needed to be taught not to expect much, and to know that the consequences of misbehavior would be nasty (hunger, homelessness, prison).[272] In that light, Hillary & Co.'s resistance to free tuition clearly has political, as well as fiscal, motives. Expectations, having been systematically beaten down for 35 years, must be beaten down further—and must not be allowed to rise.

Sometimes the "No free stuff!" imperative isn't enough and you have to resort to mockery. Paul Krugman invokes "unicorns"—he used the word six times in one column blasting Sanders' agenda.[273] *Vox* co-founder Ezra Klein characterized his single-payer plan as "puppies and rainbows."[274] Curiously, in 2007, Klein wrote a piece for *The American Prospect* reviewing the world's health care finance regimes, concluding that the U.S. should learn from "the best health-care systems in the world," including Canada's, whose system he now disdains because Sanders touts it. (Krugman included Klein's essay on a course syllabus.)[275] Austan Goolsbee, a former economic advisor to Obama who now teaches at the University of Chicago Business School and consults with hedge funds, took Klein's "puppies" up the great chain of being, saying that "they've evolved into magic flying puppies with winning Lotto tickets tied to their collars."[276]

Krugman's a funny guy. In the "unicorn" column, he pays homage to social democratic Sweden as a model society, but an actual candidate with an actual following campaigning for something like that earns nothing but condescension and mockery from him. A decade ago, Krugman told Pepe Escobar of *Asia Times* that federal revenues should be boosted to 28% of GDP from the 17% figure then.[277] It's now 19%. Then, 28% would have meant an increase of 65%; it would be a 47% increase now. Both are well above the 40% rise that Hillary's fearmongering about.

For Hillary, the fearmongering is all about keeping class discipline intact, but something else is at work with liberal intellectuals like Krugman. In a roundup of mainstream Democratic critiques of Sanders' spending proposals in the *New York Times* (where the Goolsbee magic puppies quote comes from), longtime Democratic economist Henry Aaron denounces single-payer as a "fairy tale" in the current political climate. Citing the testimony of "other economists in a 'lefty chat group' he joins online," Aaron believes that, were Sanders elected, he'd destroy his political capital by fighting such a doomed fight.

I'm familiar with this line of argument from a liberal chat group I used to hang out with online (it takes its off-the-record secrecy with great seriousness)—it may be the same one, but I can't tell for sure. It goes like this: The right so dominates the present scene that one can do nothing but play defense, hoping to salvage what remains of social spending but never daring to ask for more. Political capital, in this account, can only dwindle when put to work; unlike other forms of capital, it never pays returns. The right never thought that way when it was plotting its ascendancy from the 1950s through the 1970s.

Not content with mere fiscal sadism, Clinton and her intellectuals have gone for frank redbaiting. Among the most egregious was Paul Starr, co-founder of *The American Prospect*—the very journal where the young Ezra Klein praised single-payer. Normally the dull embodiment of tepid liberalism, Starr unleashed a raving philippic—at least by the standards of tepid liberals—aimed at Sanders.[278] Sanders is no liberal, Starr revealed—he's a socialist. He may call himself a democratic socialist, but people just say that to assure us that they're not Bolsheviks. (Starr actually says this.) Undeterred by Sanders' disavowal, Starr stokes fears of state ownership and central planning. Thankfully the word "gulag" doesn't appear in his essay, but that was probably an oversight.

Starr does have one substantial point—Sanders' tax proposals wouldn't be up to financing a Scandinavian-style welfare state. (That would require the 47% increase that Krugman once wanted.) Taxing the rich more could raise substantial revenue, but nowhere near enough. And part of the point of steepening the progressivity of the tax system is hindering great fortunes from developing and being passed on. A good part of the reason that CEO incomes have gone up so much since the early 1980s is that taxes on them have gone down; stiffen the tax on them, and there's far less incentive to pay überbosses so much in the first place. It's like taxing tobacco or carbon—you can raise revenue by doing it, but you're also trying to make the toxic things go away.

But, really, you don't need a Swedish or Danish tax structure to pay for free college tuition and single-payer health care, which are highly achievable first steps of a Sandernista political revolution. As I wrote back in 2010:

> It would not be hard at all to make higher education completely free in the USA. It accounts for not quite 2% of GDP. The personal share, about 1% of GDP, is a third of the income of the richest 10,000 households in

the U.S., or three months of Pentagon spending. It's less than four months of what we waste on administrative costs by not having a single-payer health care finance system. But introduce such a proposal into an election campaign and you would be regarded as suicidally insane.[279]

That last sentence turned out to be not a bad prophecy.

Starr really loses contact with earth when he writes about Sanders' proposal for single-payer health insurance.[280] In one sense, this is surprising, since he wrote a fat book on the history of medicine in America, and, although it was 34 years ago, is presumably still familiar with the territory. But the pressures of a political campaign often dislodge apologists' higher cerebral functions. That's the only plausible explanation for why he wrote this:

> Sanders' single-payer health plan shows the same indifference to real-world consequences. The plan calls for eliminating all patient cost sharing and promises to cover the full range of services, including long-term care. With health care running at 17.5 percent of gross domestic product, Sanders' plan would sweep a huge share of economic activity into the federal government

and invite that share to grow. Another way of looking at single payer is that it would make Washington the sole checkpoint, removing the incentive for anyone else—patients, providers, employers or state governments—even to monitor, much less hold back, excessive costs. It would leave no alternative except federal management of the health sector.

Where to start with this? Why, as a matter of principle, should patients "share costs"? They're already paying for the services with their tax dollars. According to Hillary's "skin in the game" theory, forcing patients to pay up will reduce demand, thereby keeping spending down, but this is a brutal form of cost control. Co-pays often force people to forego needed care, resulting in higher costs down the road, and more importantly, needless suffering.[281]

A far more effective form of cost control is having the government use its buying power to demand lower prices from hospitals and drug companies. That's the way it works in civilized countries, though that fact looks to have passed Starr by, probably because he was too busy trying to make precisely the opposite, and wrong, argument: single-payer would "invite that share to grow" by "removing the incentive for anyone else…even to monitor, much less hold back, excessive costs." Just what is wrong with "federal management of the health sector"? Medicare does it for the over-65 portion of the population; it works very well and is enormously popular.

Starr cites the 17.5% of GDP we devote to health care without putting that figure into any reasonable context—the sort of move that is supposed to provoke a "gee whiz" moment of surrender. According to the Organisation for Economic Co-operation and Development (OECD), a Paris-based quasi-official think tank for the world's rich countries, the U.S. spends 16.4% of GDP on health care, compared to a 10.1% average for other major countries.[282] And those other countries cover almost their entire populations, unlike the U.S., where a tenth of the population is uninsured (and many of the insured have terrible coverage), with little change since the initial drop when Obamacare first took effect. Gallup has 12% of the population uninsured, slightly higher than the Census Bureau, though with a similar trajectory of initial decline followed by flatlining.[283] Amazingly, U.S. public spending alone, 7.9% of GDP, is just 0.1 point below the international average of 8.0%. In other words, the government already spends almost as much as many other countries do while accomplishing far less. That 7.9% is also not much less than the entire health bill for Italy, Australia, and Britain, public and private combined.

Does all our spending produce better outcomes? Seems not: our life expectancy, 78.8 years, is three years shorter than the average of all the other countries.

So just about everything in Starr's quoted mini-lecture about the real world is at odds with the real world. There's a perverse form of American exceptionalism circulating around the Clinton camp: just because things work in other countries doesn't mean they can work here. As Hillary herself put it, "We are not Denmark. I love Denmark, but we are the United States of America." True enough, but that has no bearing on why single-payer couldn't work here. The only obstacles are political—elites, which include Hillary and Starr, don't want it.

The rest of Starr's piece is a highly unsubtle rant about socialism and how bad it is, even though Sanders isn't really a socialist. That sort of thing may resonate with people who grew up during the Cold War—though not with me—but it seems not to move the younger portion of the population, many of whom actually seem charmed by socialism. It's not like capitalism has been treating them all that well.

Starr also finds the style of Sanders' politics in bad taste. People like him and Krugman get uncomfortable around popular mobilizations and much prefer rule by sober technocrats. Starr complains:

Sanders is also doing what populists on both sides of the political spectrum do so well: *the mobilization of resentment.* The attacks on billionaires and Wall Street are a way of eliciting a roar of approval from angry audiences without necessarily having good solutions for the problems that caused that anger in the first place.

But people have a lot to resent—why shouldn't it be mobilized politically? And free tuition and single-payer are pretty good solutions for some of those problems. Starr just doesn't like them. Best leave the tuition issue to Hillary's vague, incomprehensible scheme (which apparently involves lots of work-study and online learning) and health care to a lightly regulated and generously subsidized insurance industry. Establishment Democrats haven't merely gone post-hope—they've declared war on it.

That war on hope may lack electoral charms, but it looks like Hillary's strategy is to pitch upmarket for November. Even though Sanders polls better against all potential Republican matchups than she does, in no small part because his politics have won over some white working-class voters, Democratic strategists seem willing to concede them in hope of luring independents and moderate Republicans (what's left of them), based on a campaign of fear against whatever ghastly option the GOP nominates. As former Pennsylvania governor Ed Rendell told the *New York Times*:

> For every one of those blue-collar Democrats [Donald Trump] picks up, he will lose to Hillary two socially moderate Republicans and independents in suburban Cleveland, suburban Columbus, suburban Cincinnati, suburban Philadelphia, suburban Pittsburgh, places like that.[284]

The strategy can be applied to Republicans other than Trump (along with Sanders, the other surprise of the 2016 campaign, which initially seemed like it would be killingly dull): terrify the moderately conservative into voting for Hillary. Forget having any positive message that might attract those disaffected "blue-collar Democrats," meaning the white working class. The appeal will be to the center-right.

Forget too the enthusiasm for Sanders among the young, an appeal based on hope for a better future. As former Obama advisor turned Uber advisor David Plouffe put it in the same *Times* article: "Hope and change, not so much. More like hate and castrate."

Maybe it will work. But this strategy of writing off the white working class is precisely what has fueled Trump's rise. As Edward Luce, the *Financial Times*' very sharp columnist, wrote:

It is the white vote—and particularly white males—that ought to worry Mrs Clinton. Blue collar whites are America's angriest people. They feel belittled, trod upon and discarded. The future belongs neither to them nor their children. Mrs Clinton personifies an establishment that has taken everything for itself while talking down to those it has left behind. Mr Trump is their revenge.[285]

Trump may or may not get the nomination. But he's emerged from and catalyzed something. And Rendell & Co.'s strategy contributes to it: if you offer resentful people no prospect for a better life, they're likely to take it out on people weaker than them.

Dems will, of course, dismiss those angry white voters as hopelessly racist and sexist. Some no doubt are, and that's the source of Trump's appeal to them. But that's not all that could appeal to them. The Sanders campaign has shown that policies that could benefit them materially have great electoral potential. But the Dem leadership would rather court suburban independents and Republicans than cross their funders.

Hillary has a lock on black voters, and it would be ugly and unproductive of me to type out a lecture on how they're mistaken in that preference. I don't understand it, but it's not my business to second-guess it. Plausible explanations I've heard for this include caution among black voters, who, fearful of the risks of a Republican presidency, gravitate towards the most "electable" Democrat; Hillary's service under a black president; identification with Hillary's "struggle"; and greater affinity for her Christian worldview than Sanders' secular, Jewish one. Whatever the reason, the Democratic establishment is playing a cynical game, relying on that "firewall" of support—voters to whom she'd offer little other than being less savage than a Republican should she take office—while they court moderate Republicans in the Columbus suburbs by running against social democracy and amping up the fear factor. Because as the man from Uber says, "Hope and change, not so much. More like hate and castrate."

There's a feeling of a collapsing old order about all this, even if Hillary does move back into the White House next January. Hillary's "electability" is frequently asserted and typically assumed, but polls do not bear this out. In most, Sanders does better against a variety of Republican opponents than she does. Such polls are hardly statistically precise, but there's really no empirical evidence of her appeal to voters. She's widely disliked, her popularity declines on exposure (it's a fact of her political life that her popularity is inversely related to her visibility), she's laden with scandals that could blow up at any moment, and she's under three federal investigations. As Ryan Lizza said of those investigations in *The New Yorker*, "However these turn out, it is unusual for a presumptive nominee and some of her current and former aides to be under investigation by the F.B.I."[286] But there's never been anything usual about Hillary.

THE FUTURE

I've paid little heed in these pages to Hillary's policy positions during this campaign. Hillary is a model of position production, but there's little reason to trust any of her proposals. I've chosen instead to look at her history, which is not inspiring. Should she become president, her administration will be little different from Obama's in its fiscal tightness and its obsession with secrecy. And, based on her time at State, it would be more likely to bomb and invade abroad.

If people want to tell me that Hillary would be a less horrid option than whatever profound ghastliness the Republicans throw up, I'll listen to them respectfully. If they try to tell me there's something inspiring or transformative about her, I'll have to wonder what planet they're on.

Yet this is too glum a note on which to conclude. A combination of Establishment propaganda, Clintonian ruthlessness, and voter caution makes it look like Hillary is more likely than not to become our next president. But the 2016 Democratic campaign, which began as what seemed like a depressing episode of eternal recurrence, got a jolt of life with the Sanders campaign, and has evolved into something that's about real politics as much as image and personality. Could it be that the wave of activism that began with Occupy Wall Street, continued with living wage protests, and has manifested itself most recently in Black Lives Matter—as frustratingly disorganized as they all were and are—is taking this electoral form now, and the future could eventually hold the possibility of something better than merely a second Clinton presidency?

HER WORDS

Here are some choice quotes from Hillary Clinton's career, some of which she probably wishes she never said. The right-wing press is full of obscenity-laced invective attributed to her. It'd be fun to include some of those—they might have deepened her charm. But I didn't fully trust the sourcing. In her book about the private lives of the First Family based on interviews with the domestic staff, The Residence, *Kate Andersen Brower does report an immense amount of "foul language" in the Clinton White House, including a celebrated moment when Hillary threw an object, probably a lamp, at Bill during the Monica Lewinsky days, with her calling him a "goddamn bastard" for emphasis.*[287]

VISION

"We are, all of us, exploring a world that none of us even understands and attempting to create within that uncertainty. But there are some things we feel, feelings that our prevailing, acquisitive, and competitive corporate life, including tragically the universities, is not the way of life for us. We're searching for more immediate, ecstatic, and penetrating modes of living."[288]

—May 1969, commencement address at Wellesley.

"I feel like my political beliefs are rooted in the conservatism that I was raised with. I don't recognize this new brand of Republicanism that is afoot now, which I consider to be very reactionary, not conservative in many respects. I am very proud that I was a Goldwater girl."[289]

—January 1991.

CLASS

"Why can't we lead the lives of normal people? They can give their daughters swimming pools; why can't we?"[290]

—To Dick Morris in the Arkansas years, no date. Hillary wanted to raise money to build a pool on the grounds of the governor's mansion. When she told Morris, he was shocked, and pointed out that the voters of a poor state would resent it immensely. He reports that despite a decent income and plenty of perks at the mansion, including prisoners as servants, she constantly felt poor and put-upon.

"You know, pushing that cart through the supermarket, and standing and talking to—I had a long conversation about clementines with the produce manager because it's been a long time since I bought a crate of clementines…[and] standing over in the dairy department trying to decide what Skim Plus meant. Because, you know, I'd never seen Skim Plus. And having a man come up to me and kind of do a double take and kind of say, 'Is that you?' and I said, 'I guess so, it is me.' It made me feel like I was re-entering the real world."[291]

—February 2000, describing a visit to a supermarket near her newly purchased $1.7 million house in Westchester just after leaving the White House.

"We came out of the White House not only dead broke, but in debt." [292]

—June 2014. The Clintons had just bought a $1.7 million Westchester house and a $2.9 million house in Washington.

"As a shareholder and director of our company, I'm always proud of Wal-Mart and what we do and the way we do it better than anybody else."[293]

—June 1990, at the annual stockholders' meeting.

"For goodness' sake, you can't be a lawyer if you don't represent banks." [294]

—March 1992. In her youth, Hillary interned at a radical law firm in Oakland, which, in Carl Bernstein's words, was "celebrated for its defense of constitutional rights, civil liberties, and leftist causes."

"Now that we've said these people are no longer deadbeats— they're actually out there being productive—how do we keep them there?"[295]

—April 2002. The "deadbeats" she's referring to are former welfare recipients who'd (briefly, in many cases) found low-wage work.

"We wanted to pass a welfare plan that would motivate and equip women to obtain a better life for themselves and their children…. I hoped welfare reform would be the beginning, not the end, of our concern for the poor…. By the time Bill and I left the White House, welfare rolls had dropped 60 percent from 14.1 million to 5.8 million, and millions of parents had gone to work…. By January 2001, child poverty had decreased by over 25 percent and was at its lowest rate since 1979. Welfare reform, the increase in the minimum wage, the reduction in taxes on low-income workers and the booming economy had moved almost eight million people out of poverty—one hundred times the number of people who left the poverty rolls during the Reagan years."[296]

—June 2003. Unfortunately, 2001 marked the low point in the poverty rate. In the following decade, poverty rates rose back to Reagan-era levels and the number of poor increased by over 13 million.

"What the fuck did we come here for? There's no money here." [297]

—During her first Senate campaign in 2000, on arriving at a campaign event in upstate New York dairy country and seeing only cows and farmers.

"I represented Wall Street, as a senator from New York." [298]

—October 2015, during the first Democratic debate.

CRIME & PUNISHMENT

"We need more police, we need more and tougher prison sentences for repeat offenders. The 'three-strikes-and-you're-out' for violent offenders has to be part of the plan. We need more prisons to keep violent offenders for as long as it takes to keep them off the streets."[299]

    —August 1994.

"I have to tell you, as I stand here, there is something wrong when a crime bill takes six years to work its way through the Congress, and the average criminal serves only four.... There will be more police on the street, a hundred thousand more police officers.... We will finally be able to say, loudly and clearly, that for repeat, violent, criminal offenders—three strikes and you're out. We are tired of putting you back in through the revolving door."[300]

    —August 1994.

"I have problems with retroactivity."[301]

    —December 2007, rejecting proposals for the reduction of sentencing disparities between crack and powdered cocaine, and for the early release of those subject to much longer sentences.

"I've got to go. The pigs are here."[302]

    —Chelsea Clinton, date unknown... bidding farewell to a friend on the phone when the Secret Service arrived to escort her to Sidwell Friends School one morning. When an agent reminded her that his job was to stand between a bullet and her family, she explained "that's what my mother and father call you." Secret

Service sources told Ronald Kessler that Chelsea generally treated the detail courteously, unlike her parents.

"Fuck off." [303]

—Late 1990s. Response to a Secret Service agent who'd said "good morning" during the Monica Lewinsky days.

WAR & PEACE

"In the four years since the inspectors [left], intelligence reports show that Saddam Hussein has worked to rebuild his chemical and biological weapons stock, his missile delivery capability, and his nuclear program. He has also given aid, comfort, and sanctuary to terrorists, including al-Qaida members.... If left unchecked, Saddam Hussein will continue to increase his capacity to wage biological and chemical warfare, and will keep trying to develop nuclear weapons. Should he succeed in that endeavor, he could alter the political and security landscape of the Middle East, which as we know all too well affects American security." [304]

—October 2002, on floor of U.S. Senate.

"It's time for the United States to start thinking of Iraq as a business opportunity."[305]

—June 2011, to an audience of senior executives from U.S. companies and officials from the U.S. and Iraqi governments.

"U.S. policy must be clear and unequivocal: We cannot, we should not, we must not, permit Iran to build or acquire nuclear weapons. In dealing with this threat…no option can be taken off the table."[306]

—February 2007.

"I want the Iranians to know that if I'm the president, we will attack Iran (if it attacks Israel). In the next 10 years, during which they might foolishly consider launching an attack on Israel, we would be able to totally obliterate them."[307]

—April 2008.

"I remember landing under sniper fire. There was supposed to be some kind of a greeting ceremony at the airport, but instead we just ran with our heads down to get into the vehicles to get to our base."[308]

—March 2008, describing her landing in Bosnia. This was an invention; there was no sniper fire.

"We came, we saw, he died."[309]

—October 2011, on the death of Muammar Qaddafi.

"[I]n a conflict like this, the hard men with the guns are going to be the more likely actors in any political transition than those on the outside just talking."[310]

—August 2014, on the need to arm the Syrian rebels, describing a position she took as the nation's top diplomat.

TRADE

"I think everybody is in favor of free and fair trade. I think NAFTA is proving its worth."

—March 1996, at a union event.

"There was a very effective business effort in the United States on behalf of NAFTA. There was a very limited and ineffective effort on behalf of fast track. I don't know all the reasons for that…. For whatever reason, the fact that the American business community made a very limited effort on behalf of the fast track, left the field completely clear to the rather unusual alliance between the right of the Republican party, which is isolationist, anti-American engagement, quite critical and not supportive of the United Nations, IMF or any multilateral group, and the left of the Democratic party that believes that trade authority, and trade agreements are not in the interests of American workers. So that alliance carried the day. Now when the President comes back to the Congress with a request for fast track authority I hope that American business voices will be heard."

—February 1998, at the World Economic Forum, Davos.

"What happened to NAFTA, I think, was we inherited an agreement that we didn't get everything we should have got out of it in my opinion. I think the NAFTA agreement was flawed."

—March 2000, before the Working Families Party.

"Creating a free trade zone in North America—the largest free trade zone in the world—would expand U.S. exports, create jobs and ensure that our economy was reaping the benefits, not the burdens, of globalization. Although unpopular with labor unions, expanding trade opportunities was an important administration goal."

—2003, from *Living History*.

"I think on balance NAFTA has been good for New York and America…."

—January 2004.

"As I have said for months, I oppose the deal. I have spoken out against the deal, I will vote against the deal, and I will do everything I can to urge the Congress to reject the Colombia Free Trade Agreement."

—April 2008.

"First, let me underscore President Obama's and my commitment to the [Colombia] Free Trade Agreement. We are going to continue to work to obtain the votes in the Congress to be able to pass it. We think it's strongly in the interests of both Colombia and the United States. And I return very invigorated…to begin a very intensive effort to try to obtain the votes to get the Free Trade Agreement finally ratified."[311]

—June 2010.

"During my tenure as Senator, I have voted for every trade agreement that has come before the Senate and I believe that properly negotiated trade agreements can increase living standards and foster openness and economic development for all parties."[312]

—June 2005.

WHISTLEBLOWING

"I think turning over a lot of that material—intentionally or unintentionally—drained, gave all kinds of information, not only to big countries, but to networks and terrorist groups and the like. So I have a hard time thinking that somebody who is a champion of privacy and liberty has taken refuge in Russia, under Putin's authority."[313]

—April 2014, on Edward Snowden's release of documents revealing the vast spying operations of the National Security Agency.

EMAILS

"You may have seen that I recently launched a Snapchat account. I love it. I love it. Those messages disappear all by themselves."[314]

—August 2015.

"I don't know, I have no idea. Like with a cloth or something?"[315]

—August 2015. Days after the joke above, in response to a question about whether she'd "wiped" her email server.

ABORTION

"It is a violation of human rights when women are denied the right to plan their own families."

—September 1995.

"I have said many times that I can support a ban on late-term abortions, including partial-birth abortions, so long as the health and life of the mother is protected."

—October 2000; later, she voted against a bill to ban partial-birth abortions.

"I for one respect those who believe with all their heart and conscience that there are no circumstances under which abortion should be available." [316]

—January 2005.

MARRIAGE

"Marriage has got historic, religious and moral content that goes back to the beginning of time, and I think a marriage has always been between a man and a woman."

—January 2000.

"[Marriage is] a sacred bond between a man and a woman."

—January 2004.

"Well, I prefer to think of it as being very positive about civil unions. You know, it's a personal position. How we get to full equality is the debate we're having, and I am absolutely in favor of civil unions with full equality of benefits, rights, and privileges."

—August 2007, responding to a question about why she was opposed to same-sex marriage.

"LGBT Americans are our colleagues, our teachers, our soldiers, our friends, our loved ones. And they are full and equal citizens, and they deserve the rights of citizenship. That includes marriage. That's why I support marriage for lesbian and gay couples. I support it personally and as a matter of policy and law, embedded in a broader effort to advance equality and opportunity for LGBT Americans and all Americans." [317]

—March 2013.

HISTORY

"It may be hard for your viewers to remember how difficult it was for people to talk about HIV/AIDS back in the 1980s. And because of both President and Mrs. Reagan, in particular Mrs. Reagan, we started a national conversation, when before nobody would talk about it, nobody wanted to do anything about it. That too is something that I really appreciate with her very effective, low-key advocacy, but it penetrated the public conscience and people began to say, 'Hey, we have to do something about this….'"

—March 2016, interview with Andrea Mitchell. Some conversation they started. In fact, as *Teen Vogue* put it in a provocative but accurate headline, "Former First Lady Nancy Reagan watched thousands of LGBTQ people die of AIDS." Despite her influence with her husband, she didn't intervene as the disease ravaged her friends in the worlds of Hollywood and fashion; his administration did nothing and his press secretary laughed off questions about the topic. When her friend Rock Hudson was dying of AIDS in 1985, he requested her help in getting experimental treatment in France; she turned down his request.[318] Hours after saying this, Hillary apologized.

"I don't know where [Bernie Sanders] was when I was trying to get health care in '93 and '94." [319]

—March 2016. Actually, she wrote him a thank-you note for his "commitment to real health care access for all Americans" beneath a photo of them talking in 1993. C-SPAN has (user-supplied) video of Sanders standing behind her as she spoke at a press conference, also in 1993, promoting her health reform effort; she thanked him for his support.[320]

DIVERSITY

"I am, you know, adamantly against illegal immigrants. We've got to do more at our borders. And people have to stop employing illegal immigrants." [321]

—February 2003. During the 2008 campaign, she was criticized for a vague, equivocating stance on giving driver's licenses to undocumented immigrants, a policy she now supports, along with a "path to citizenship" for those who are already here.

"They should be sent back as soon as it can be determined who responsible adults in their families are…." [322]

—June 2014, speaking of unaccompanied children crossing into the United States from Mexico. Most of the children were fleeing extreme circumstances and would be well positioned to claim humanitarian relief under U.S. law.

"I love this quote. It's from Mahatma Gandhi. He ran a gas station in Saint Louis for a few years." [323]

—January 2004. She later apologized.

"Senator Obama's support among working, hard-working Americans, white Americans, is weakening again." [324]

—May 2008, during the primary campaign.

CHARACTER

"The office of the president is such that it calls for a higher level of conduct than expected from the average citizen of the United States."[325]

—Written in 1974, as a staff lawyer drawing up the rules for the impeachment of Richard Nixon.

"I'm not sitting here like some little woman standing by her man like Tammy Wynette. I'm sitting here because I love him and I honor what he's been through and what we've been through together."[326]

—January 1992, *60 Minutes* interview.

"If I didn't kick his ass every morning, he'd never amount to anything." [327]

—Date unknown, about her husband.

"[Bill is a] hard dog to keep on the porch."[328]

—August 1999.

"People should and do trust me."[329]

—July 2015.

AN AUTHOR'S NOTE ABOUT THIS BOOK'S COVER

As the first edition of this book was entering production, we circulated the cover to get people talking about it. We never imagined how successful that strategy would be.

The Washington Post and *Cosmopolitan* both wrote about the cover. On Twitter, former Obama speechwriter turned screenwriter Jon Lovett called it "gross." *Nation* pundit Joan Walsh called it "disgusting." *Salon* writer Amanda Marcotte diagnosed "issues with women" (the author's, apparently, not the artist's). Writing in *New York* magazine, Rebecca Traister proposed that the image shows how "a competent professional woman...can be so intimidating that her menace is best portrayed as a violent threat." The right even took notice, with the cover featured on the front of *Drudge* and a link to an MSNBC.com story about the controversy (one of several meta-stories about the cover's reception). The *Drudge* link described me as a "lib," which is a cruel slur.

Tweets and think-pieces about the cover quickly became a subgenre of a larger argument that tries to portray tough criticism of Hillary as sexist—inevitably so, given its incorporation into a dominant patriarchal discourse, regardless of the author's position. One of the cover's critics who also read the book—the only one of the commenters who did, as far as I know—conceded that there's nothing sexist in it, but identified the fundamental problem as my inability to see the election of a woman president in itself as a significant feminist goal in itself.

It would be a good thing to have a woman president after the 43 bepenised ghouls and functionaries who've occupied the office. (OK, there were a few who weren't half-bad—you wouldn't need more than one hand to count them.) But, as I argue in this book, if you're looking for a more peaceful, more egalitarian society you'd have to overlook a lot about Hillary's history to develop any enthusiasm for her. The side of feminism I've studied and admired for decades has been about moving towards that ideal, and not merely placing women into high places while leaving the overall hierarchy of power largely unchanged. It's distressing to see feminism pressed into service to promote the career of a thoroughly orthodox politician—and the charge of sexism used to deflect critiques of her.

It was also distressing to read interpretations of Sarah Sole's painting on the cover that were, as the writer Tracy Quan put it in a radio interview, "middlebrow," "philistine," and "moralistic." When I first stumbled on Sarah's work—scores of paintings and collages involving Hillary in various poses, ranging from the amorous to the violent—via Facebook a few years ago, I was drawn to it despite my lack of fondness for its subject. Sarah explained that she had a real libidinal fixation on Hillary. At first I thought that she had some sort of ironic relation to that fixation but she eventually convinced me that she really didn't. When it came to thinking of cover art for this book I suggested her work to Colin Robinson, the "R" in OR Books, precisely because of its power and its capacity to stir interest. I also thought it would be interesting to have a cover exist in some sort of tension with the book, a point lost on some of its critics, who seem more comfortable with straightforward agitprop. Colin agreed, and selected the gun-toting image.

Just how is the cover sexist? To me, it shows Hillary's ruthlessness and especially her hawkishness—features of her history that were detailed in the book—though spiced up with Sarah Sole's libidinal obsession. To Hillary's defenders, making that point is inevitably sexist, a position that would make nearly any serious criticism of her impossible. Her hawkishness is well—established, from her eagerness to get on the Armed Services Committee on arrival in the Senate, to her vote for the Iraq war, to her out-hawking Defense Secretary Robert Gates while serving as our top diplomat, to her call for bringing in "the hard men with the guns" to solve the problems of Syria, a country already overwhelmed by men with guns.

But the Hillary camp reads the cover as expressing anxiety about powerful and ambitious women. (That's certainly not the artist's intent, but of course art has a life of its own beyond what its creator thought it meant.) I am fine with powerful and ambitious women. It's what they do with that power and ambition that concerns me. In Hillary's case, she's largely used it to support the existing order rather than challenge it. I do wonder, though, whether the suggestion of Hillary's bellicosity reminds some of her supporters of something they'd rather not think about her.

There's no doubt that Hillary has been the target of all kinds of vicious sexist attacks during her decades in public life. They're vile, and have no place in any political critique. I can't stop people from appropriating the cover or the book to some misogynist agenda, but I won't miss an opportunity to condemn those who do, because it's a distraction from the indictment of her long record that follows once you open the book.

ACKNOWLEDGMENTS

This book originated as an article for *Harper's* magazine.[330] I'd like to thank the publisher, Rick MacArthur, whose idea it was for me to write the piece; James Marcus, the editor who worked with me on it; Camille Bromley, who fact-checked it; Giulia Melucci, who publicized it; and others whose names I didn't learn but who helped as well. They have been wonderful to work with in every respect.

I'd also like to thank Colin Robinson of OR Books, who asked me to expand that article into this broadside. This is my third book with Colin, who is not only an excellent publisher but also a very good friend. Thanks as well to Dan Simon and his colleagues at Seven Stories for transforming this into a trade book so quickly. For assistance on the Haiti portion of the story, I'd like to thank Greg Higgins and Nikolas Barry-Shaw. And many thanks as well to Sam Miller for research (and friendship).

The Hillary literature is vast but uneven. Some of the plentiful right-wing critiques are unhinged and unreliable, and I've mostly avoided them for reasons of credibility (doubting theirs and protecting mine). On the sane side of the spectrum, though,

I want to single out three books as particularly fine sources: Jeff Gerth and Don Van Natta's *Her Way*, Carl Bernstein's *A Woman in Charge*, and Gail Sheehy's *Hillary's Choice*.

With its sleek dimensions, this book may look footnote-heavy, but Hillary's defenders are fervent. When my *Harper's* article appeared, Correct the Record, an HRC front group run by her former-enemy-turned-ceaseless-defender David Brock, posted a widely ignored 9,000-word refutation of it—a voluminous response to a 6,000-word piece. (The refutation now looks to have been taken down, but Michelle Goldberg wrote about it in her profile of Brock in *The Nation*.)[331] Similarly, but less volubly, Joe Conason—who apparently performs his strenuous Hillary apologetics purely out of love—also wrote an instant refutation, focusing largely on a few hundred words I wrote about Whitewater, which were entirely correct and survived the magazine's rigorous fact-checking, and overlooking the rest of the damning story.[332] Conason couldn't get over the fact that I'd quoted Dick Morris, who admittedly has some strange beliefs, but who also has a sharp political mind. (Conason & Co. find Morris thoroughly disreputable, forgetting, or perhaps remembering, that he was on the Clinton payroll for 20 years.) No doubt these grunts in the Hillary army will be scrutinizing this book for errors, and that's why I've provided plenty of footnotes for their interns to work with. I look forward to their reviews.

On a happier note, I'd like to thank my wife, Liza Feather-stone, who is the love of my life and a crucial part of everything I do. I hope our son, Ivan, will inherit a world where people better than Hillary Clinton rise to prominence.

NOTES

1. Brad DeLong, "Time to pound my head against the wall once again," *The Semi-Daily Journal of Economist Brad DeLong*, June 7, 2003. <https://web.archive.org/web/20030611041719/http://www.j-bradford-delong.net/movable_type/2003_archives/001600.html>.

2. Dan Gonyea, "'How's That Hopey, Changey Stuff?' Palin Asks," NPR, February 7, 2010 <http://www.npr.org/templates/story/story.php?storyId=123462728>.

3. Quoted in Jeff Gerth and Dale Van Natta, *Her Way: The Hopes and Ambitions of Hillary Rodham Clinton* (New York: Little, Brown and Co., 2007), Kindle loc. 2942.

4. Dick Morris, *Rewriting History* (New York: HarperCollins, 2009), p. 134.

5. "Public Faith in Congress Falls Again, Hits Historic Low," http://www.gallup.com/poll/171710/public-faith-congress-falls-again-hits-historic-low.aspx.

6. Matt Stoller, "Obama's admiration of Ronald Reagan," *Open Left*, January 16, 2008 <http://www.openleft.com/showDiary.do?diaryId=3263>; "In their own words: Obama on Reagan," *New York Times*, n.d. <http://www.nytimes.com/ref/us/

politics/21seelye-text.html>.

7. William F. Martin and George Cabot Lodge, "Our society in 1985—business may not like it," *Harvard Business Review*, November-December 1975, pp. 143–150.

8. I owe this point to my friend Heather Gautney.

9. U.S. Treasury, "Major foreign holdings of Treasury securities," September 16, 2015 <http://www.treasury.gov/ticdata/Publish/mfh.txt>.

10. Morris, *Rewriting History*, p. 34.

11. Hillary Rodham Clinton, *It Takes a Village* (New York: Simon & Schuster, 2006), Kindle loc. 355–357.

12. Ibid., Kindle loc. 426–427.

13. Carl Bernstein, *A Woman in Charge*, (Knopf, 2007), Kindle loc. 9381–9382.

14. Ibid., Kindle loc. 11722–11723.

15. Gail Sheehy, *Hillary's Choice* (Random House, 2000), Kindle loc. 650–658; David Maraniss, *First in His Class: A Biography of Bill Clinton* (Simon & Schuster, 1995), Kindle loc. 4834.

16. Sheehy, *Hillary's Choice,* Kindle loc. 665–675.

17. Ibid., Kindle loc. 686.

18. Ibid., Kindle loc. 862.

19. Ibid., Kindle loc. 885–910.

20. Ibid., Kindle loc. 925.

21. Sheehy, *Hillary's Choice*, Kindle loc. 997. Maraniss, *First in His Class*, Kindle loc. 4877.

22. Interview with NPR's *Weekend Edition*, January 13, 1996. Audio at <https://www.youtube.com/watch?v=h15-tiVWk-0>.

23. Sheehy, *Hillary's Choice*, Kindle loc. 1169–1173.

24. Ibid., Kindle loc. 1329.

25. Ibid., Kindle loc. 1378.

26. Maraniss, *First in His Class*, Kindle loc. 4996.

27. Hillary Rodham, "There is only the fight…" (Wellesley senior thesis), chap. 1, near footnote 23 <http://www.economicpolicyjournal.com/2013/04/hillary-clintons-1969-thesis-on-saul.html>.

28. Hillary D. Rodham's 1969 Student Commencement Speech <http://www.wellesley.edu/events/commencement/archives/1969commencement/studentspeech>.

29. Bill Clinton, speech to the National Realtors Association, April 27, 1993, White House official transcript <http://www.presidency.ucsb.edu/ws/index.php?pid=46486>. The White House transcription spelled the poet's name as "Sandberg."

30. Sheehy, *Hillary's Choice*, Kindle loc. 1607.

31. Bernstein, *A Woman in Charge*, Kindle loc. 1612–1614.

32. Maraniss, *First in His Class*, Kindle loc. 4787.

33. Ibid., Kindle loc. 4803.

34. Ibid., Kindle loc. 4819.

35. Bernstein, *A Woman in Charge*, Kindle loc. 1278.

36. Quoted in Duncan Lindsey and Rosemary Sarri, "What Hillary Rodham Clinton Really Said About Children's Rights and Child Policy," *Children and Youth Services Review* 14 (1992), p. 476. <http://deepblue.lib.umich.edu/bitstream/handle/2027.42/30351/0000753.pdf?sequence=1>.

37. Bernstein, *A Woman in Charge*, Kindle loc. 9695.

38. Melinda Henneberger, "Will Hillary Clinton run against her husband's welfare legacy," *Bloomberg*, May 26, 2015 <http://www.bloomberg.com/politics/articles/2015-05-26/will-hillary-clinton-run-against-her-husband-s-welfare-legacy->.

39. Maraniss, *First in His Class*, Kindle loc. 5825–5828.

40. Sheehy, *Hillary's Choice*, Kindle loc. 2106–2107. Maraniss, *First in His Class*, Kindle loc. 6140.

41. Bernstein, *A Woman in Charge*, Kindle loc. 1754–1755.

42. Ibid., Kindle loc. 2246–2247.

43. Ibid., Kindle loc. 1860–1862.

44. Maraniss, *First in His Class*, Kindle loc. 6187.

45. Ibid., Kindle loc. 6769.

46. Ibid., Kindle loc. 6847.

47. Gerth and Van Natta, *Her Way*, Kindle loc. 1095–1116.

48. Bernstein, *A Woman in Charge*, Kindle loc. 1665, 1668–1669.

49. Maraniss, *First in His Class*, Kindle loc. 7840–7870.

50. Ibid., Kindle loc. 8030.

51. Ibid., Kindle loc. 8105.

52. Bernstein, *A Woman in Charge*, Kindle loc. 3505.

53. Maraniss, *First in His Class*, Kindle loc. 8216.

54. Bernstein, *A Woman in Charge*, Kindle loc. 3621–3625.

55. Maraniss, *First in His Class*, Kindle loc. 9004.

56. Sheehy, *Hillary's Choice*, Kindle loc. 4308–4315. Transcript of address to DLC at <http://www.edb.utexas.edu/visionawards/ptl/sti2012/files/DC_STI_Session5Readings.pdf>.

57. Sheehy, *Hillary's Choice*, Kindle loc. 3489–3490.

58. Michael Barbaro, "As director, Clinton moved Wal-Mart

board, but only so far," *New York Times*, May 20, 2007 <http://www.nytimes.com/2007/05/20/us/politics/20walmart.html?pagewanted=all>.

59. Brian Ross, Maddy Sauer, and Rhonda Schwartz, "Clinton remained silent as Wal-Mart fought unions," ABC News, January 31, 2008 <http://abcnews.go.com/Blotter/story?id=4218509>.

60. Sheehy, *Hillary's Choice*, Kindle loc. 3576–3603. Gerth and Van Natta, *Her Way*, Kindle loc. 1485–1492.

61. Maraniss, *First in His Class*, Kindle loc. 8710.

62. Gerth and Van Natta, *Her Way*, Kindle loc. 1698–1702.

63. Bernstein, *A Woman in Charge*, Kindle loc. 4746–4754.

64. Ibid., Kindle loc. 6308.

65. Hillary Clinton, *Living History* (Simon & Schuster, 2003), p. 292.

66. Ibid., Kindle loc. 6595–6596.

67. Ibid., Kindle loc. 6470–6478.

68. Raymond Hernandez, "With a step right, Senator Clinton agitates the left," *New York Times*, May 22, 2002 <http://www.nytimes.com/2002/05/22/nyregion/with-a-step-right-senator-clinton-agitates-the-left.html>.

69. Center on Budget and Policy Priorities, "Chart Book: TANF at 18" <http://www.cbpp.org/cms/?fa=view&id=3566>.

70. Bernstein, *A Woman in Charge*, Kindle loc. 8705–8719, 9391–9396, 9403; Mary B.W. Tabor, "Meet Hillary Rodham Clinton, the traditional First Lady," *New York Times*, April 22, 1995 <http://www.nytimes.com/1995/04/22/us/meet-hillary-rodham-clinton-the-traditional-first-lady.html >; Barbara Feinman Todd, "Ghost writing," *The Writer's Chronicle*, September 2002 <https://www.

awpwrit-er.org/magazine_media/writers_chronicle_view/1603>; Doreen Carvajal, "On book tour, Mrs. Clinton defends herself," *New York Times*, January 14, 1996 <http://www.nytimes. com/1996/01/14/us/on-book-tour-mrs-clinton-defends-herself.html >; Susan Threadgill, "Who's Who," *Washington Monthly*, June 1999 <http://www.washingtonmonthly.com/ other/1999/9906.ww.html>.

71. Gerth and Van Natta, *Her Way*, Kindle loc. 2394.

72. Ibid., Kindle loc. 1229.

73. Though now probably forgotten, the S&L crisis of the 1980s was a major financial trauma of the early neoliberal era. Originally conceived of as sleepy institutions that took deposits from small savers and lent that money conservatively for home mortgages, they were deregulated in the early 1980s. The deregulation was in part a response to the troubles the industry was experiencing with the high interest rates of the time—their portfolio of long-term mortgages were at fixed, low interest rates, but to attract deposits, they needed to pay higher rates, well above what they were making on the mortgages. Deregulation was supposed to fix the problem by allowing them to compete aggressively for deposits and enter new lines of supposedly more lucrative business, like commercial real estate, which would earn higher returns. The strategy didn't work out. Management was too unsophisticated to play with the big boys and made a lot of bad loans. By the end of the decade, the S&L business was in deep trouble, with about a third of institutions going under by the mid-1990s. Resolving the crisis required the expenditure of hundreds of billions of Federal

dollars—no one actually knows how much. Twenty years later, it would be dwarfed by the mortgage crisis of 2007–2008, but at the time it seemed like a massive crisis whose only precedent was the wave of bank failures of the early 1930s.

74. Gerth and Van Natta, *Her Way*, Kindle loc. 2111–2120, 2127–2141.

75. Ibid., Kindle loc. 2990.

76. Ibid., Kindle loc. 3032–3033.

77. Ibid., Kindle loc. 3053.

78. Bernstein, *A Woman in Charge*, Kindle loc. 5403.

79. Gerth and Van Natta, *Her Way*, Kindle loc. 3879–3892, 3946.

80. Adam Nagourney, "Mrs. Clinton vows fight on issues and image," *New York Times*, February 6, 2000 <http://www.nytimes.com/2000/02/06/nyregion/mrs-clinton-vows-fight-on-issues-and-image.html>.

81. Daniel Halper, *Clinton, Inc.: The Audacious Rebuilding of a Political Machine* (New York: HarperCollins, 2014), Kindle loc. 1475–1477.

82. Kathryn Joyce and Jeff Sharlet, "Hillary's prayer: Hillary Clinton's religion and politics," *Mother Jones*, September 2007 <http://www.motherjones.com/politics/2007/09/hillarys-prayer-hillary-clintons-religion-and-politics?page=4>.

83. Halper, *Clinton, Inc.*, Kindle loc. 1474–1490, 1635.

84. Joyce and Sharlet, "Hillary's prayer."

85. Gerth and Van Natta, *Her Way*, Kindle loc. 4638.

86. Gerth and Van Natta, *Her Way*, Kindle loc. 5568.

87. In the late 1990s and early 2000s, I interviewed Elizabeth

Warren on my radio show several times, and corresponded and talked with her frequently about the politics and economics of bankruptcy reform. Her 1989 book, *As We Forgive Our Debtors*, co-written with Teresa A. Sullivan and Jay Lawrence Westbrook, was a rigorous and original study of the causes and effects of bankruptcy that did severe empirical damage to the credit industry's claims that those who file for relief are immoral deadbeats. Warren recounted her briefing of Hillary in a 2004 interview with Bill Moyers that's available at <https://www.youtube.com/watch?v=12mJ-U76nfg>. There's background at Emma Roller, "How Hillary Clinton once disappointed Elizabeth Warren on Wall Street reform," *National Journal*, September 5, 2014 <http://www.nationaljournal.com/politics/2014/09/05/How-Hillary-Clinton-Once-Disappointed-Elizabeth-Warren-Wall-Street-Reform>.

88. Laura Meckler, "Hillary Clinton's explanation for controversial bankruptcy vote? Joe Biden," *Wall Street Journal*, September 17, 2015 <http://blogs.wsj.com/washwire/2015/09/17/hillary-clintons-explanation-for-controversial-bankruptcy-vote-joe-biden/>. For Biden's history with MBNA and the industry in general, see Eric Umansky, "Biden's cozy relations with bank industry," *ProPublica*, August 25, 2008 <https://www.ProPublica.org/article/bidens-cozy-relations-with-bank-industry-825>.

89. <http://obsidianwings.blogs.com/obsidian_wings/2008/02/solutions-adden.html>; <http://obsidianwings.blogs.com/obsidian_wings/2008/02/but-wait-theres.html>.

90. Associated Press, "Clinton seeks 'Grand Theft Auto' probe," *USA Today*, July 14, 2005 <http://usatoday30.usatoday.com/news/washing ton/2005-07-14-clinton-game_x.htm>; Family Entertainment Protection Act, *GovTrack*, December 16, 2005 <https://www.govtrack.us/congress/bills/109/s2126>.

91. Clinton, *It Takes a Village*, Kindle loc. 3450–3452.

92. Unsigned editorial, "Senator Clinton, in pander mode," *New York Times*, December 7, 2005 <http://www.nytimes.com/2005/12/07/opinion/senator-clinton-in-pander-mode.html>.

93. Bills sponsored or cosponsored by Senator Hillary Rodham Clinton <https://www.congress.gov/member/hillary-clinton/C001041?resultIndex=1&q=%7B%22search%22%3A%5B%22hil.

94. DemocraticLuntz (pseudonym), "Hillary Clinton voted to continue cluster bombing civilians," *Daily Kos*, December 21, 2007 <http://m.dailykos.com/story/2007/12/21/425303/->; roll call vote: <http://www.senate.gov/legislative/LIS/roll_call_lists/roll_call_vote_cfm.cfm?congress=109&session=2&vote=00232>; texts of Feinstein amendment, SA 4882, and brain injury amendment, SA 4883: <http://thomas.loc.gov/cgi-bin/query/D?r109:3:./temp/~r109r4FAm9>.

95. Derek Willis, "The Senate votes that divided Hillary Clinton and Bernie Sanders," *New York Times*, May 27, 2015 <http://www.nytimes.com/2015/05/28/upshot/the-senate-votes-that-divided-hillary-clinton-and-bernie-sanders.html>; Amber Phillips, "Yes, Bernie Sanders voted to kill immigration reform in 2007. But it's complicated," *Washington Post*, March 10, 2016 <https://www.washingtonpost.com/news/the-fix/wp/2016/03/10/yes-bernie-

sanders-voted-to-kill-immigration-reform-in-2007-but-its-
complicated/>.

96. Gerth and Van Natta, *Her Way*, Kindle loc. 4080–4081, 4104.

97. Bob Dreyfuss, "An idea factory for the Democrats," *The Nation*,
March 1, 2004 <http://www.thenation.com/article/idea-factory-
democrats/>.

98. Ken Silverstein, "The secret donors behind the Center for
American Progress and other think tanks," *The Nation*, June
10, 2013 <http://www.thenation.com/article/secret-donors-
behind-center-american-progress-and-other-think-tanks-
updated-524/>.

99. Greg Sargent, "Center for American Progress, poised to wield
influence over 2016, reveals its top donors," Washington Post,
January 21, 2015 <https://www.washingtonpost.com/blogs/plum-
line/wp/2015/01/21/center-for-american-progress-poised-to-
wield-influence-over-2016-reveals-its-top-donors/>.

100. Ben Smith, "Soros gives to Media Matters, publicly," Politico,
October 20, 2010 <http://www.politico.com/blogs/ben-
smith/2010/10/soros-gives-to-media-matters-publicly-030089>.

101. Jim VandeHei and Chris Cillizza, "A new alliance of Democrats
spreads funding," *Washington Post*, July 17, 2006 <http://www.
washingtonpost.com/wp-dyn/content/article/2006/07/16/
AR2006071600882_pf.html>.

102. Chuck Todd, "Calling out Media Matters bias," *NBC News*,
November 15, 2007 <http://firstread.nbcnews.com/_
news/2007/11/15/4429164-calling-out-media-matters-bias>.

103. John Heilemann and Mark Halperin, *Game Change* (New York:

Harper, 2010), pp. 33–34, 90.

104. Ibid., p. 92.

105. Ibid., p. 165.

106. For the text of the ad, see Ariel Alexovich, "Clinton's national security ad," *New York Times*, February 29, 2008 <http://thecaucus.blogs.nytimes.com/2008/02/29/clintons-national-security-ad/?_r=0>. For video, see <https://www.youtube.com/watch?v=7yr7odFUARg>.

107. Angie Drobnic Holan, "Video shows tarmac welcome, no sniper fire," *PolitiFact.com,* March 25, 2008 <http://www.politifact.com/truth-o-meter/statements/2008/mar/25/hillary-clinton/video-shows-tarmac-welcome-no-snipers/>.

108. Robert Yoon, "Disclosure reports show Clinton still deeply in debt," *CNN*, August 22, 2008 <http://politicalticker.blogs.cnn.com/2008/08/22/disclosure-reports-show-clinton-still-deeply-in-debt/>.

109. Kathy Kiely and Jill Lawrence, "Clinton makes case for wide appeal," *USA Today*, May 8, 2008 <http://usatoday30.usatoday.com/news/politics/election2008/2008-05-07-clintoninterview_N.htm>.

110. Joshua Green, "The front-runner's fall," *The Atlantic*, September 2008 <http://www.theatlantic.com/magazine/archive/2008/09/the-front-runner-s-fall/306944/>.

111. "List of U.S. states by African–American population," *Wikipedia* <https://en.wikipedia.org/wiki/List_of_U.S._states_by_African-American_population#African-American_proportion_of_state_populations_.281790-2010.29>.

112. Heilemann and Halperin, *Game Change*, p. 214.

113. Amy Chozick, "Frank discussions on race help define Hillary Clinton's 2016 campaign," *New York Times*, June 22, 2015 <http://www.nytimes.com/2015/06/23/us/politics/hillary-clinton-embraces-racial-issues-in-departure-from-2008.html>. Bill's stature-diminishing comments were so frequent that Politico compiled a list of "Bill Clinton's 8 digs at Obama," September 5, 2012 <http://www.politico.com/news/stories/0912/80728.html>.

114. Xuan Thai and Ted Barrett, "Biden's description of Obama draws scrutiny," CNN, February 9, 2007 <http://www.cnn.com/2007/POLITICS/01/31/biden.obama/>.

115. Quoted in Heilemann and Halperin, *Game Change*, p. 146.

116. <http://correctrecord.org/11-things-you-should-know-about-hillary/>.

117. B'Tselem, "Gaza Strip," August 12, 2014 <http://www.btselem.org/gaza_strip/20140812_preliminary_data_on_fatalities>.

118. Pew Research Center, "Global Opinion of Obama Slips" <http://www.pewglobal.org/2012/06/13/global-opinion-of-obama-slips-international-policies-faulted/>.

119. Eli Sugarman, "5 Top Highlights in Hillary Clinton's Secretary of State Tenure," *Policy.Mic*, January 2, 2013 <http://mic.com/articles/21829/5-top-highlights-in-hillary-clinton-s-secretary-of-state-tenure>.

120. Paul Richter, "Hillary Clinton's legacy at State: Splendid but not spectacular," *Los Angeles Times*, January 28, 2013 <http://articles.latimes.com/2013/jan/28/nation/la-na-clinton-legacy-20130128>. The text is considerably more modest than

the "splendid" in the headline would suggest.

121. Michael Gordon and Mark Landler, "Backstage glimpses of Clinton as dogged diplomat, win or lose," *New York Times*, February 2, 2013 <http://www.nytimes.com/2013/02/03/us/ politics/in-behind-scene-blows-and-triumphs-sense-of-clinton- future.html>.

122. Stephen M. Walt, "Is Hillary Clinton a great Secretary of State?," *Foreign Policy*, July 10, 2012 <http://foreignpolicy. com/2012/07/10/is-hillary-clinton-a-great-secretary-of-state/>.

123. Michael S. Schmidt, "Hillary Clinton used personal email account at State Department, possibly breaking rules," *New York Times*, March 2, 2015 <http://www.nytimes.com/2015/03/03/ us/politics/hillary-clintons-use-of-private-email-at-state- department-raises-flags.html>; Peter Nicholas and Laura Meckler, "Clinton private email plan drew concerns early on," *Wall Street Journal*, March 11, 2015 <http://www.wsj.com/ articles/clinton-private-email-plan-drew-concerns-early- on-1426117692>; Philip Bump, "Hacked e-mails indicate that Hillary Clinton used a domain registered the day of her Senate hearings," *Washington Post*, March 2, 2015 <http://www. washingtonpost.com/news/the-fix/wp/2015/03/02/hacked- emails-indicate-that-hillary-clinton-used-a-domain-registered- the-day-of-her-senate-hearings/>.

124. U.S. Department of State, Office of the Inspector General, "About OIG" <https://oig.state.gov/about>.

125. Byron Tau and Peter Nicholas, "State Department lacked top watchdog during Hillary Clinton tenure," *Wall Street*

Journal, March 24, 2015 <http://www.wsj.com/articles/state-department-lacked-top-watchdog-during-hillary-clinton-tenure-1427239813>.

126. Shushannah Walshe and Liz Kreutz, "Hillary Clinton's deleted emails were individually reviewed after all, spokesman says," ABC News, March 15, 2015 <http://abcnews.go.com/Politics/hillary-clintons-deleted-emails-individually-reviewed-spokesman/story?id=29654638>.

127. Peter Baker, "Emails show Hillary Clinton trying to find her place," *New York Times*, July 1, 2015 <http://www.nytimes.com/2015/07/02/us/politics/emails-show-hillary-clinton-trying-to-find-her-place.html>.

128. Michael S. Schmidt, "Benghazi emails put focus on Hillary Clinton's encouragement of adviser," *New York Times*, June 29, 2015 <http://www.nytimes.com/2015/06/30/us/politics/benghazi-emails-put-focus-on-hillary-clintons-encouragement-of-adviser.html>.

129. Kenneth P. Vogel, "Clinton Foundation paid Blumenthal $10K a month while he advised on Libya," *Politico*, May 28, 2015 <http://www.politico.com/story/2015/05/clinton-foundation-sidney-blumenthal-salary-libya-118359.html>.

130. Jonathan Alter, "Schwarzman: 'It's a war' between Obama, Wall St.," *Newsweek*, August 15, 2010 <http://www.newsweek.com/schwarzman-its-war-between-obama-wall-st-71317>.

131. Zachary Mider, "Wall Street's Hillary Clinton: E-mails take a different tone toward financiers," *Bloomberg Politics*, July 2, 2015 <http://www.bloomberg.com/politics/articles/2015-07-02/wall-

street-s-hillary-clinton-e-mails-take-a-different-tone-towards-
financiers>.

132. Charles R. Babcock, "Hillary Clinton futures trades detailed,"
Washington Post, May 27, 1994 <https://www.washingtonpost.
com/wp-srv/politics/special/whitewater/stories/wwtr940527.
htm>.

133. Raymond Hernandez, "Weiner's wife didn't disclose consulting
work she did while serving in State Dept.," *New York Times*,
May 16, 2013 <http://www.nytimes.com/2013/05/17/nyregion/
weiners-wife-huma-abedin-failed-to-disclose-consulting-work-
done-while-a-state-dept-aide.html>.

134. Maggie Haberman, John Bresnahan, and Glenn Thrush,
"Huma Abedin allowed to represent clients while at State,"
Politico, May 16, 2013 <http://dyn.politico.com/printstory.
cfm?uuid=156E8E80-6478-42CA-A205-B2D089F6A2C7>;
Justin Elliott and Liz Day, "Who are State Dept's 100 'Special
Government Employees'? It won't say," *ProPublica*, November
13, 2013 <http://www.*ProPublica*.org/article/state-wont-reveal-
special-government-employees-huma-abedin>; Justin Elliott
and Liz Day, "State Department finally releases list of 'special
government employees,'" *ProPublica*, January 30, 2014 <http://
www.*ProPublica*.org/article/state-department-finally-releases-
list-of-special-government-employees>. The SGE story was told
accurately by Peter Schweizer, but I cite sources other than him to
keep David Brock's formidable hair in place.

135. Alec McGillis, "Scandal at Clinton Inc.," *The New Republic*,
September 22, 2013 <http://www.newrepublic.com/

article/114790/how-doug-band-drove-wedge-through-clinton-dynasty>.

136. Tom Huddleston Jr., "Consulting firm Teneo is betting big on Britain," *Fortune*, July 9, 2015 <http://fortune.com/2015/07/09/teneo-acquisition-blue-rubicon-stockwell/>.

137. "About Teneo" <http://www.teneoholdings.com/about/>.

138. Hillary Clinton, "America's Pacific Century," *Foreign Policy*, October 11, 2011 <http://foreignpolicy.com/2011/10/11/americas-pacific-century/>.

139. Christopher Bodeen, "China criticizes US force strengthening in Asia," Associated Press, *The Irrawaddy*, April 17, 2013 <http://www.irrawaddy.org/asia/china-criticizes-us-force-strengthening-in-asia.html>. For details on the U.S. military buildup, see U.S. Navy, *A Cooperative Strategy for 21st Century Seapower*, March 2015 <http://www.navy.mil/local/maritime/150227-CS21R-Final.pdf>.

140. Hillary Clinton, *Hard Choices* (New York: Simon & Schuster, 2014), p. 79.

141. "Secretary Jewell applauds passage of U.S.–Mexico Transboundary Hydrocarbons Agreement," U.S. Department of the Interior press release, December 23, 2013 <http://www.doi.gov/news/pressreleases/secretary-jewell-applauds-passage-of-us-mexico-transboundary-hydrocarbons-agreement.cfm>.

142. Steve Horn, "Exclusive: Hillary Clinton State Department emails, Mexico energy reform, and the revolving door," *DeSmog*, August 7, 2015 <http://www.desmogblog.com/2015/08/07/hillary-clinton-state-department-emails-mexico-energy-reform-revolving-door>; Carlos Pascual, "Transboundary

reservoirs—a window of opportunity," *WikiLeaks*, August 17, 2009 <https://cablegatesearch.wikileaks.org/cable. php?id=09MEXICO2445&q=and%20and%20and%20energy%20 mexico%20pascual%20reform>.

143. Alexander Main, "Hillary Clinton's emails and the Honduras coup," *The Americas Blog*, September 23, 2015 < http://cepr. net/blogs/the-americas-blog/the-hillary-clinton-emails-and- honduras>.

144. Lee Fang, "During Honduras crisis, Clinton suggested back channel with lobbyist Lanny Davis," *First Look*, July 6, 2015 <https://firstlook.org/theintercept/2015/07/06/clinton- honduras-coup/>; Justin Elliott, "Lanny Davis' African human rights disaster," *Salon*, January 5, 2011 <http://www.salon. com/2011/01/05/lanny_davis_equatorial_guinea/>.

145. Roberto Lovato, "Our man in Honduras," *The American Prospect*, July 22, 2009 <http://prospect.org/article/our-man-honduras>. Email: <https://foia.state.gov/searchapp/DOCUMENTS/ HRCEmail_August_Web/IPS-0098/DOC_0C05771340/ C05771340.pdf>.

146. Clinton, *Hard Choices*, pp. 265–267.

147. Belén Fernández, "Hillary does Honduras," in *False Choices: The Faux Feminism of Hillary Rodham Clinton*, ed. Liza Featherstone (New York and London: Verso, 2016), p. 139.

148. Email from Greg Grandin to me, July 21, 2015.

149. Greg Grandin, "Before her murder, Berta Cáceres singled out Hillary Clinton for criticism," *The Nation*, March 10, 2016 <http://www.thenation.com/article/chronicle-of-a-honduran-

assassination-foretold/>.

150. That assumes $250,000 for a one-hour speech, which works out to $4,167 per minute, or $69 per second. Haiti's per capita income, according to the World Bank, is $810 <http://data.worldbank.org/country/haiti>.

151. Jonathan M. Katz, "The King and Queen of Haiti," *Politico*, May 4, 2015 <http://www.politico.com/magazine/story/2015/05/clinton-foundation-haiti-117368_full.html>.

152. Clinton, *Hard Choices*, p. 528.

153. Bill Clinton, *My Life* (New York: Knopf, 2004), Kindle loc. 4731.

154. Allan Nairn, "Aristide banks on austerity," *Multinational Monitor*, August 1994 <http://www.multinationalmonitor.org/hyper/issues/1994/08/mm0894_05.html>; Helen Scott and Ashley Smith, "Behind Aristide's fall," Socialist Worker, March 12, 2004 <http://socialistworker.org/2004-1/490/490_06_Aristide.shtml>; Ives Marie Chanel, "Haiti: Clock ticking on structural adjustment decision," InterPress Service, September 28, 1995 <http://www.williambowles.info/haiti-news/archives/structural_adj_280995.html>; InterPress Service, "Haiti: Prime minister pledges fidelity to economic plan," September 8, 1995 <http://www.williambowles.info/haiti-news/archives/pm_080995.html>.

155. Katz, "The King and Queen of Haiti."

156. Dan Coughlin and Kim Ives, "WikiLeaks Haiti: Let them live on $3 a day," *The Nation*, June 1, 2011 <http://www.thenation.com/article/161057/wikileaks-haiti-let-them-live-3-day>.

157. Adam Davidson, "Would a $5-a-day minimum wage make life better in Haiti?," *Planet Money,* June 8, 2011 <http://www.

npr.org/sections/money/2011/06/10/137064161/would-a-5-a-day-minimum-wage-make-life-better-in-haiti>. Davidson interview with me: <http://www.leftbusinessobserver.com/Radio.html#S120609>.

158. Dan Coughlin and Kim Ives, "WikiLeaks Haiti: Cable depicts fraudulent Haiti election," *The Nation*, June 8, 2011 <http://www.thenation.com/article/161216/wikileaks-haiti-cable-depicts-fraudulent-haiti-election>.

159. Email from Cheryl Mills, March 20, 2011 <http://graphics.wsj.com/hillary-clinton-email-documents/#/?docid=C05779428>.

160. Yamiche Alcindor, "High hopes for Hillary Clinton, then disappointment in Haiti," *New York Times*, March 14, 2016 <http://www.nytimes.com/2016/03/15/us/politics/hillary-clinton-haiti.html?_r=0>.

161. Trenton Daniel, "Haiti pres [sic], Clinton form board to court investors," *Associated Press*, September 8, 2011 <http://finance.yahoo.com/news/Haiti-pres-Clinton-form-board-apf-2417127420.html>.

162. Amelie Baron, "Disorder, delays mar Haiti's long-awaited election," *AFP*, August 10, 2015 <http://news.yahoo.com/violence-low-turnout-threaten-haitis-sunday-elections-035425298.html>.

163. Frances Robles, "Haitian leader's power grows as scandals swirl," *New York Times*, March 16, 2015 <http://www.nytimes.com/2015/03/17/world/americas/haitian-president-tightens-grip-as-scandal-engulfs-circle-of-friends.html>.

164. Frances Robles, "Michel Martelly, Haiti's president, departs

without a successor," *New York Times*, February 7, 2016 <http://www.nytimes.com/2016/02/08/world/americas/michel-martelly-haitis-president-departs-without-a-successor.html>.

165. Curiously, the only concrete force contributing to recovery that Hillary mentioned was "the great resilience and strength of the Haitian people." Hillary Rodham Clinton, "Remarks to the press, Port-au-Prince, Haiti," January 16, 2010 <http://www.state.gov/secretary/20092013clinton/rm/2010/01/135278.htm>.

166. Hillary Rodham Clinton, "Update on developments in Haiti," January 20, 2010 <http://www.state.gov/secretary/20092013clinton/rm/2010/01/135461.htm>.

167. Mike McIntire and Steve Eder, "Roger Clinton is wary, chatty, and still occasionally attracting attention," *New York Times*, July 6, 2015 <http://www.nytimes.com/2015/07/07/us/politics/clinton-first-brother-is-wary-chatty-and-still-occasionally-attracting-attention.html>; Steve Eder, "Tony Rodham's Ties Invite Scrutiny for Hillary and Bill Clinton," *New York Times*, May 10, 2015 <http://www.nytimes.com/2015/05/11/us/politics/tony-rodhams-ties-invite-scrutiny-forhillary-and-bill-clinton.html>.

168. For the relationship between USAID and the State Department see U.S. Diplomacy, "Agency for International Development (USAID)" <http://www.usdiplomacy.org/state/abroad/usaid.php> and U.S. Department of State, "Department of State and USAID Strategic Plan" <http://www.state.gov/s/d/rm/rls/dosstrat/>.

169. "With poor track records for-profit development companies team up to fight reform," *Haiti Relief and Reconstruction Watch*, December 1, 2011 <http://cepr.net/blogs/haiti-relief-and-

reconstruction-watch/with-poor-track-records-for-profit-development-companies-team-up-to-fight-reform>.

170. Jacqueline Charles, "Hillary Clinton–backed post-quake Haiti project 'a work in progress,'" *Miami Herald*, May 3, 2015 <http://www.miamiherald.com/news/nation-world/world/americas/haiti/article20129688.html>.

171. Greg Higgins, "Architectural Peer Review of Caracol EKAM Housing, Haiti – March 16, 2012" <http://www.hrdf.org/files/Architectural-Peer-Review-Caracol-EKAM-Haiti_2012mar16.pdf>.

172. Email from Greg Higgins to me, July 2, 2015.

173. Isabel Macdonald and Isabeau Doucet, "The shelters that Clinton built," *The Nation*, August 1–8, 2011 <http://www.thenation.com/article/shelters-clinton-built/>.

174. Kevin Sullivan and Rosalind S. Helderman, "How the Clintons' Haiti development plans succeed—and disappoint," *Washington Post*, March 20, 2015 <http://www.washingtonpost.com/politics/how-the-clintons-haiti-development-plans-succeed--and-disappoint/2015/03/20/0ebae25e-cbe9-11e4-a2a7-9517a3a70506_story.html>; Jonathan O'Connell, "In Haiti, a Marriott's opening is the latest milestone in quake recovery," *Washington Post*, February 26, 2015 <http://www.washingtonpost.com/business/capitalbusiness/in-haiti-a-marriotts-opening-is-the-latest-milestone-in-quake-recovery/2015/02/26/bc3cadde-bd0e-11e4-8668-4e7ba8439ca6_story.html>.

175. I. Lomholt, "Sorg Architects designs new staff housing for the U.S. embassy in Haiti," *e-architect*, January 6, 2012 <http://www.e-

architect.co.uk/haiti/us-embassy-housing-haiti>.

176. The Department of State's original request for proposals can be found at <https://www.fbo.gov/index?s=opportunity&mode=form&id= 52485fe7117ae4189638ff76249e8da3&tab=core&_cview=1>. Artists' renditions of the project can be found at <http://www. worldarchitecturenews.com/wanmobile/mobile/article/18642>. For pictures of the original Bidonvilles, see <http://www.pbase.com/ jpsuriha/bidonville>. A State Department spokesperson said the housing, which initially was supposed to have been completed in 2014, was still under construction in September 2015. It took some persistence to confirm whether the proposed housing was actually built, suggesting that it might be an embarrassing legacy of the Hillary era. A call to the embassy in Port-au-Prince was not returned, though presumably almost anyone working in the building could have answered the question. It took several calls and emails before the State Department finally confirmed that construction was underway.

177. Jonathan M. Katz, "The Clintons' Haiti screw-up, as told by Hillary's emails," *Politico*, September 2, 2015 <http://www.politico. com/magazine/story/2015/09/hillary-clinton-email-213110>.

178. Jeffrey Goldberg, "Hillary Clinton: 'Failure' to Help Syrian Rebels Led to the Rise of ISIS" <http://www.theatlantic.com/ international/archive/2014/08/hillary-clinton-failure-to-help- syrian-rebels-led-to-the-rise-of-isis/375832/>.

179. Mark Landler, "A Rift in Worldviews Is Exposed as Clinton Faults Obama on Policy," *New York Times*, August 11, 2014 <http://www. nytimes.com/2014/08/12/world/middleeast/attacking-obama- policy-hillary-clinton-exposes-different-worldviews.html>.

180. Jacob Heilbrunn, "The Next Act of the Neocons," *New York Times*, July 5, 2014 <http://www.nytimes.com/2014/07/06/opinion/sunday/are-neocons-getting-ready-to-ally-with-hillary-clinton.html>.

181. Josh Rogin, "Victoria Nuland to be State Department Spokesman" <http://thecable.foreignpolicy.com/posts/2011/05/16/victoria_nuland_to_be_state_department_spokesman>; Jonathan Marcus, "Ukraine crisis: transcript of leaked Nuland–Pyatt call," BBC, February 7, 2014 <http://www.bbc.com/news/world-europe-26079957>.

182. Michael Crowley, "Hillary Clinton's unapologetically hawkish record faces 2016 test," *Time*, January 14, 2014 <http://swampland.time.com/2014/01/14/hillary-clintons-unapologetically-hawkish-record-faces-2016-test/>.

183. Chris Smith, "Here Hillary stands," *New York*, July 10, 2006 <http://nymag.com/news/politics/citypolitic/17399/>.

184. "Dick Cheney heaps praise on Hillary Clinton," *The Telegraph*, September 5, 2011 <http://www.telegraph.co.uk/news/worldnews/us-politics/8741148/Dick-Cheney-heaps-praise-on-Hillary-Clinton.html>.

185. Scott Shane and Jo Becker, "Hillary Clinton, 'smart power' and a dictator's fall," *New York Times*, February 27, 2016 <http://www.nytimes.com/2016/02/28/us/politics/hillary-clinton-libya.html>; Scott Shane and Jo Becker, "A new Libya, with 'very little time left,'" *New York Times*, February 27, 2016 <http://www.nytimes.com/2016/02/28/us/politics/libya-isis-hillary-clinton.html>.

186. Rebecca Ballhaus, "Charts: The Clintons' well-oiled fundraising

machine," *Wall Street Journal*, July 2, 2014 <http://blogs.wsj.com/washwire/2014/07/02/charts-the-clintons-well-oiled-fundraising-machine/>; Brody Mullins, Peter Nicholas, and Rebecca Ballhaus, "The Bill and Hillary Clinton money machine taps corporate cash," *Wall Street Journal*, July 1, 2014 <http://www.wsj.com/articles/the-bill-and-hillary-clinton-money-machine-taps-corporate-cash-1404268205>.

187. Philip Rucker, Tom Hamburger, and Alexander Becker, "How the Clintons went from 'dead broke' to rich: Bill earned $104.9 million for speeches," *Washington Post*, June 26, 2014 <http://www.washingtonpost.com/politics/how-the-clintons-went-from-dead-broke-to-rich-bill-earned-1049-million-for-speeches/2014/06/26/8fa0b372-fd3a-11e3-8176-f2c941cf35f1_story.html>.

188. "The net worth of American presidents: Washington to Obama," *24/7 Wall Street*, May 10, 2010 (with updates) <http://247wallst.com/banking-finance/2010/05/17/the-net-worth-of-the-american-presidents-washington-to-obama/>. Their list is helpfully sorted by Wikipedia, at <https://en.wikipedia.org/wiki/List_of_United_States_Presidents_by_net_worth>. I computed the partisan averages. The median net worth of Democratic presidents in 2010 dollars was $18 million; of Republicans, $6 million. Before rounding that yields a 3.2/1 ratio. Mean net worth is higher for both party averages, as is usually the case for wealth figures; that ratio is 6.1 times, again in favor of Democrats. The Dems' mean is pulled substantially higher by John F. Kennedy, whose family worth was a billion dollars at current prices. Excluding JFK from

the mean still leaves Democratic presidents 1.9 times as rich as their Republican counterparts. To figure the averages, when the net worth was listed as less than $1 million, I imputed the value of $500,000. This affects five Republicans and three Democrats—Dems dominate the high end, and Reps have the edge on the low end.

189. Annie Karni and Isabelle Taft, "Fear of debt drove Clinton's dash for cash," *Politico*, September 18, 2015 <http://www.politico.com/story/2015/09/hillary-clinton-candidate-wealth-2016-213317>.

190. Geoff Earle, "Bill Clinton foundation has spent more than $50M on travel expenses," *New York Post*, August 20, 2013 <http://nypost.com/2013/08/20/bill-clinton-foundation-has-spent-more-than-50m-on-travel-expenses/>.

191. Anne E. Kornblut, "What's in a Murdoch-Clinton alliance? Something for both sides," *New York Times*, May 10, 2006 <http://www.nytimes.com/2006/05/10/nyregion/10hillary.html>; Patricia Sellers, "The *Fortune* interview: Rupert Murdoch," *Fortune*, April 10, 2014 <http://fortune.com/2014/04/10/the-fortune-interview-rupert-murdoch/>.

192. Rebecca Ballhaus, "Charts: The Clintons' well-oiled fundraising machine," *Wall Street Journal*, July 2, 2014 <http://blogs.wsj.com/washwire/2014/07/02/charts-the-clintons-well-oiled-fundraising-machine/>.

193. Michael Tomasky, "The Hillary in Our Future," *New York Review of Books*, June 25, 2015.

194. Peter Schweizer, *Clinton Cash: The Untold Story of How and Why Foreign Governments and Businesses Helped Make Bill and Hillary*

Rich (New York: HarperCollins, 2015), Kindle loc. 2837–2841.

195. Lauren Carroll, "Fact-checking 'Clinton Cash' author on claim about Bill Clinton's speaking fees," *PolitiFact*, April 26, 2015 <http://www.politifact.com/punditfact/statements/2015/apr/26/peter-schweizer/fact-checking-clinton-cash-author-claim-about-bill/>; Matthew Mosk and Brian Ross, "Bill Clinton cashed in when Hillary became Secretary of State," ABC News, April 23, 2015 <http://abcnews.go.com/Politics/bill-clinton-cashed-hillary-secretary-state/story?id=30522705>.

196. Pratap Bhanu Mehta, "Charity at home?," *Indian Express*, October 19, 2010 <http://archive.indianexpress.com/news/charity-at-home-/699359/0>.

197. James V. Grimaldi and Rebecca Ballhaus, "Hillary Clinton's complex corporate ties," *Wall Street Journal*, February 19, 2015 <http://www.wsj.com/articles/hillary-clintons-complex-corporate-ties-1424403002>.

198. Clinton, *Hard Choices*, p. 509.

199. Jo Becker and Don Van Natta Jr., "After mining deal, financier donated to Clinton," *New York Times*, January 31, 2001 <http://www.nytimes.com/2008/01/31/us/politics/31donor.html?pagewanted=all>; Anu Narayanswamy, "Travels with Bill and Frank: A look at the Clinton-Giustra friendship," *Washington Post*, May 3, 2015 <http://www.washingtonpost.com/news/post-politics/wp/2015/05/03/travels-with-bill-and-frank-a-look-at-the-clinton-giustra-friendship/>.

200. Clinton, *Hard Choices*, pp. 237, 238, 554.

201. Jo Becker and Mike McIntire, "Cash flowed to Clinton

Foundation amid Russian uranium deal," *New York Times*, April 23, 2015 <http://www.nytimes.com/2015/04/24/us/cash-flowed-to-clinton-foundation-as-russians-pressed-for-control-of-uranium-company.html>; Mike McIntire and Jo Becker, "Canadian partnership shielded identities of donors to Clinton Foundation," *New York Times*, April 29, 2015 <http://www. nytimes.com/2015/04/30/us/politics/canadian-partnership-shielded-identities-of-donors-to-clinton-foundation.html>.

202. James V. Grimaldi and Rebecca Ballhaus, "UBS deal shows Clinton's complicated ties," *Wall Street Journal*, July 30, 2015 <http://www.wsj.com/articles/ubs-deal-shows-clintons-complicated-ties-1438223492>.

203. Gillian B. White, "The empty promises of for-profit colleges," *The Atlantic*, September 15, 2015 <http://www.theatlantic. com/business/archive/2015/09/the-failure-of-for-profit-colleges/405301/>.

204. "Clinton sought invite for Laureate at State Dept. dinner," *Inside Higher Ed*, September 2, 2015 <https://www.insidehighered. com/quicktakes/2015/09/02/clinton-sought-invite-laureate-state-dept-dinner>; Hillary email: <https://foia.state.gov/searchapp/DOCUMENTS/HRCEmail_JulyWeb/Web_031/DOC_0C05763085/C05763085.pdf>.

205. Richard Rubin and Jennifer Epstein, "Hillary and Bill Clinton made $139 million in eight years," *Bloomberg Politics*, July 31, 2015 <http://www.bloomberg.com/politics/articles/2015-07-31/hillary-and-bill-clinton-paid-43-million-in-federal-taxes>.

206. Mina Kimes and Michael Smith, "Laureate, a for-profit education

firm, finds international success (with a Clinton's help)," *Washington Post*, January 18, 2014 <https://www.washingtonpost. com/business/laureate-a-for-profit-education-firm-finds- international-success-with-a-clintons-help/2014/01/16/13f8adde- 7ca6-11e3-9556-4a4bf7bcbd84_story.html>.

207. Clinton Health Access Initiative, Inc., *Consolidated Financial Statements, December 31, 2013 and 2012* <http://45.55.138.94/ content/uploads/2015/05/Clinton-Health-Access-Initiative- Financial-Statements-2013.pdf>.

208. Clinton Health Access Initiative, Inc., *IRS Form 990*, 2013, p. 2 <http://45.55.138.94/content/uploads/2015/05/Clinton-Health- Access-Initiative-Inc-2013-Form-990-Schedule-B-omitted-.pdf>.

209. Clinton Health Access Initiative, Inc., *Annual Report 2013* <http://45.55.138.94/content/uploads/2015/05/CHAI_Annual_ Report_2013.pdf>.

210. PEPFAR, 2009 *Annual Report to Congress* <http://www.pepfar. gov/documents/organization/113827.pdf>.

211. Kaiser Family Foundation, "The U.S. President's Emergency Plan for AIDS Relief (PEPFAR)," June 4, 2014 <http://kff.org/global- health-policy/fact-sheet/the-u-s-presidents-emergency-plan-for/>.

212. Sudarsan Raghavan and David Nakamura, "Bush AIDS policies shadow Obama in Africa," *Washington Post*, June 30, 2013 <https://www.washingtonpost.com/world/africa/bush-aids- policies-shadow-obama-in-africa/2013/06/30/0c8e023c-e1ac- 11e2-aef3-339619eab080_story.html>.

213. Nicholas Confessore and Amy Chozick, "Unease at the Clinton Foundation over finances and ambitions," *New York Times*,

August 13, 2013 <http://www.nytimes.com/2013/08/14/us/
politics/unease-at-clinton-foundation-over-finances-and-
ambitions.html>.

214. Lyrics provided by Gogola.

215. Dylan Byers and Maggie Haberman, "Chelsea Clinton paid $600k
by NBC," Politico, June 13, 2014 <http://www.politico.com/
story/2014/06/chelsea-clinton-nbc-600-k-salary-107827.html>.

216. Amy Chozick, "Chelsea Clinton, living up to the family name," *New
York Times*, December 3, 2011 <http://www.nytimes.com/2011/12/04
/fashion/chelsea-clinton-living-up-to-the-family-name.html>.

217. Philip Rucker and Rosalind S. Helderman, "A college balks
at Hillary Clinton's fee, books Chelsea for $65,000 instead,"
Washington Post, June 30, 2015 <http://www.washingtonpost.
com/politics/a-college-balks-at-hillary-clintons-fee-so-books-
chelsea-for-65000-instead/2015/06/29/b1918e42-1e78-11e5-
84d5-eb37ee8eaa61_story.html>.

218. Joe Dziemianowicz, "Chelsea Clinton's lavish, star-studded wedding
ceremony will cost between $3 million and $5 million," *New
York Daily News*, July 27, 2010 <http://www.nydailynews.com/
entertainment/gossip/chelsea-clinton-lavish-star-studded-wedding-
ceremony-cost-3-million-5-million-article-1.441179>; Regina
Medina, "Pop the questions on Chelsea's wedding," Philadelphia
Daily News, July 30, 2010 <http://articles.philly.com/2010-07-30/
news/24971000_1_wedding-chelsea-clinton-guests>.

219. Richard Johnson, "Staff quit Clinton Foundation over Chelsea,"
New York Post, May 18, 2015 <http://pagesix.com/2015/05/18/
chelsea-sends-clinton-foundation-staff-running/>.

220. Kenneth P. Vogel and Noah Weiland, "Clinton Foundation snubbed by the pope, Elton John, Janet Yellen," *Politico*, September 26, 2015 <http://www.politico.com/story/2015/09/clinton-foundation-snubbed-pope-elton-john-janet-yellen-214091>; David Mastio, "Obama admin, big businesses abandon Clinton Global Initiative," *USA Today*, September 19, 2015 <http://www.usatoday.com/story/opinion/2015/09/18/clinton-foundation-sponsor-dow-exxon-hp-samsung-hsbc-hp-mastio-column/72336094/>.

221. Interview with Dick Morris.

222. Bernstein, *A Woman in Charge*, Kindle loc. 5117–5118.

223. Ruby Cramer, "Hillary speeds through parade, ignores protesters, ropes off the press—and insists she's having fun," *BuzzFeed*, July 5, 2015 <http://www.buzzfeed.com/rubycramer/hillary-out-of-her-comfort-zone-speeds-through-parade-ignore>.

224. "Hillary Clinton's presidential campaign announcement (official)," ABC News, April 12, 2015 <https://www.youtube.com/watch?v=N708P-A45D0>.

225. Amy Chozick, "Middle class is disappearing, at least from vocabulary of possible 2016 contenders," *New York Times*, May 11, 2015 <http://www.nytimes.com/2015/05/12/us/politics/as-middle-class-fades-so-does-use-of-term-on-campaign-trail.html>.

226. Matt Viser, "Warren plans Israel trip after midterm elections," *Boston Globe*, August 13, 2014 <https://www.bostonglobe.com/news/politics/2014/08/13/elizabeth-warren-has-skimpy-resume-foreign-policy-but-plans-israel-trip-after-mid-terms/6gkD7HBwuQlHuUrgeMDB0I/story.html>.

227. Video at <https://www.youtube.com/watch?v=bzhEkHzIUno&feature=youtu.be>.

228. Glenn Greenwald, "Elizabeth Warren finally speaks on Israel/Gaza, sounds like Netanyahu," *The Intercept*, August 28, 2014 <https://firstlook.org/theintercept/2014/08/28/elizabeth-warren-speaks-israelgaza-sounds-like-netanyahu/>.

229. "Lucrative side business: Hillary Clinton raises eyebrows after netting $400K giving two speeches at Goldman Sachs," *Daily Mail*, October 31, 2013 <http://www.dailymail.co.uk/news/article-2482262/Hillary-Clinton-nets-400K-2-speeches-Goldman-Sachs.html>.

230. Heather Digby Parton, "Hillary shocker: Who needs Elizabeth Warren? Clinton unleashes inner liberal, media freaks out," *Salon*, June 8, 2015 <http://www.salon.com/2015/06/08/hillary_shocker_who_needs_elizabeth_warren_clinton_unleashes_inner_liberal_media_freaks_out/>.

231. Josh Voorhees, "Why Hillary Clinton has moved so far and so fast to the left," *Slate*, June 8, 2015 <http://www.slate.com/blogs/the_slatest/2015/06/08/hillary_clinton_runs_left_why_the_democratic_frontrunner_is_embracing_the.html>.

232. Dara Lind, "Why Bernie Sanders doesn't talk about race," *Vox*, May 27, 2015 <http://www.vox.com/2015/5/27/8671135/bernie-sanders-race>.

233. Seth Ackerman, "What are the most important issues for people of color?," *Too Hot for Jacobin*, June 1, 2015 <http://toohotforjacobin.blogspot.com/2015/06/what-are-most-important-issues-for.html>.

234. Ben Schreckinger and Annie Karni, "Hillary Clinton's criminal justice plan: reverse Bill's policies," *Politico*, April 29, 2015 <http://www.politico.com/story/2015/04/hillary-clintons-criminal-justice-plan-reverse-bills-policies-117488.html>; Andrew Kaczynski, "Here's Hillary Clinton in 1994 talking up tough-on-crime legislation," *BuzzFeed*, April 29, 2015 <http://www.buzzfeed.com/andrewkaczynski/times-change-heres-hillary-clinton-in-1994-talking-up-tough>.

235. Joan Walsh, "Did this man cost the Democrats the election?," *Salon*, November 5, 2004 <http://www.salon.com/2004/11/06/gay_marriage_19/>; Joan Walsh, "White progressives' racial myopia: Why their colorblindness fails minorities—and the left," *Salon*, June 1, 2015 <http://www.salon.com/2015/06/01/white_progressives_racial_myopia_why_their_colorblindness_fails_minorities_and_the_left/>.

236. Douglas A. Berman, "Clinton campaign assails Obama for advocating against federal mandatory minimums," *Sentencing Law and Policy*, January 5, 2008 <http://sentencing.typepad.com/sentencing_law_and_policy/2008/01/clinton-aides-a.html>; "Is Senator Clinton to the right of Justice Scalia on sentencing issues?," December 12, 2007 <http://sentencing.typepad.com/sentencing_law_and_policy/2007/12/is-senator-clin.html>.

237. Stephen Gillers, "Hillary Clinton's Ethical Challenge," *The Nation*, June 9, 2015 <http://www.thenation.com/article/209497/hillary-clintons-ethical-challenge>

238. Rebecca Traister, "Meet the New, Old Hillary," *The New Republic,* June 14, 2015 <http://www.newrepublic.com/article/122035/

meet-new-old-hillary-clinton>.

239. Rebecca Traister, "I'm a hot mess for Hillary," *Elle*, October 1, 2015 <http://www.elle.com/culture/career-politics/a30203/hillary-clinton-hot-mess/>.

240. Daisy Benson, "If it's truly progressive, Labour will have voted in a female leader—regardless of her policies," *The Independent*, September 11, 2015 <http://www.independent.co.uk/voices/if-its-truly-progressive-labour-will-have-voted-in-a-female-leader-regardless-of-her-policies-10496237.html>. See also Suzanne Moore, "As Jeremy Corbyn was annointed leader, not one female voice was heard," *The Guardian*, September 12, 2015 <http://www.theguardian.com/politics/2015/sep/12/jeremy-corbyn-not-one-female-voice> (Moore apparently didn't notice that Corbyn got the majority of women's votes); and Cathy Newman, "Welcome to Jeremy Corbyn's blokey Britain—where 'brocialism' rules," *The Telegrap*h, September 14, 2015 <http://www.telegraph.co.uk/women/womens-life/11863186/Welcome-to-Jeremy-Corbyns-blokey-Britain-where-brocialism-rules.html>.

241. Anthony Weiner, "I have one big question for Bernie," *Business Insider* <http://www.businessinsider.com/anthony-weiners-question-for-bernie-sanders-2015-7>.

242. Nicholas Confessore and Maggie Haberman, "Hillary Clinton lags in engaging grass-roots donors," *New York Times*, July 15, 2015 <http://www.nytimes.com/2015/07/16/us/politics/hillary-clinton-lags-in-engaging-grass-roots-donors.html>.

243. Rebecca Ballhaus, "Hillary Clinton raised $28 million in 3rd quarter, edging Bernie Sanders," *Wall Street Journal*, September

30, 2015 <http://www.wsj.com/articles/hillary-clinton-raised-28-million-in-3rd-quarter-edging-bernie-sanders-1443665690>.

244. Rebecca Ballhaus, "Bernie Sanders doubled his fundraising haul in February," *Wall Street Journal*, February 29, 2016 <http://blogs.wsj.com/washwire/2016/02/29/bernie-sanders-doubled-his-fundraising-haul-in-february/>.

245. Anne Gearan and Matea Gold, "Clinton on blitz to post big fundraising number next week; holds party at home of 'Barbarians at the Gate' financier," *Washington Post*, September 26, 2015 <http://www.washingtonpost.com/news/post-politics/wp/2015/09/26/clinton-on-blitz-to-post-big-fundraising-number-next-week-holds-party-at-home-of-barbarians-at-the-gate-financier/>.

246. Evan Halper and Melanie Mason, "Hillary Clinton's big donors in California have found all sorts of reasons to be nervous," *Los Angeles Times*, September 27, 2015 <http://www.latimes.com/nation/politics/la-na-clinton-california-donors-20150925-story.html>.

247. Fredreka Schouten and Christopher Schnaars, "Hundreds of Obama bundlers missing from Clinton's elite fundraising ranks," *USA Today*, October 18, 2015 <http://www.usatoday.com/story/news/politics/elections/2016/2015/10/18/hundreds-obama-bundlers-missing-clintons-elite-fundraising-ranks/74170182/>.

248. For useful histories of the 2008 campaign, see Suzanne Goldenberg, "How Hillary Clinton turned an air of certainty into a losing run," *The Guardian*, June 3, 2008 <http://

www.theguardian.com/world/2008/jun/04/hillaryclinton.
uselections20084> and Joshua Green, "The front-runner's fall,"
The Atlantic, September 2008 <http://www.theatlantic.com/
magazine/archive/2008/09/the-front-runner-s-fall/306944/>.

249. Ed O'Keefe and John Wagner, "100,000 people have come to
recent Bernie Sanders rallies. How does he do it?," *Washington
Post*, August 11, 2015 <https://www.washingtonpost.com/
politics/how-does-bernie-sanders-draw-huge-crowds-to-see-
him/2015/08/11/4ae018f8-3fde-11e5-8d45-d815146f81fa_story.
html>.

250. Sam Frizell, "The gospel of Bernie," *Time*, September 17, 2015
<http://time.com/4038080/the-gospel-of-bernie/>.

251. Zeke J. Miller, "Clinton jokes about email investigation," *Time*,
August 14, 2015 <http://time.com/3999368/hillary-clinton-
emails-investigation-joke/>.

252. Annie Karni, "Allies fault Hillary Clinton's response on
emails," *Politico*, August 19, 2015 <http://www.politico.
com/story/2015/08/allies-fault-hillary-clinton-response-on-
emails-121509.html>.

253. Rosalind S. Helderman, Tom Hamburger, and Carol D. Leonnig,
"Tech company: No indication that Clinton's e-mail server was
'wiped,'" *Washington Post*, September 12, 2015 <http://www.
washingtonpost.com/politics/tech-company-no-indication-that-
clintons-e-mail-server-was-wiped/2015/09/12/10c8ce52-58c6-
11e5-abe9-27d53f250b11_story.html>.

254. Glenn Thrush and Hadas Gold, "David Brock: The *New York
Times* has 'a special place in hell,'" Politico, September 10, 2015

<http://www.politico.com/story/2015/09/david-brock-new-york-times-hell-213484>.

255. Gabriel DeBenedetti and Nick Gass, "Clinton: I'm 'sorry' the email scandal is confusing to people," Politico, September 4, 2015 <http://www.politico.com/story/2015/09/hillary-clinton-private-email-no-apologies-213349>.

256. Maggie Haberman, "Hillary Clinton, citing her 'mistake,' apologizes for private email," *New York Times*, September 8, 2015 <http://www.nytimes.com/politics/first-draft/2015/09/08/hillary-clinton-calls-private-email-server-a-mistake-says-im-sorry-about-that/>.

257. Bigtree, "There are marked differences in Martin O'Malley's response to BLM activists' challenge," *Democratic Underground*, August 9, 2015 <http://www.democraticunderground.com/1251504574>.

258. Kevin Rector, "O'Malley's presidential announcement comes amid revived criticism of policing policies," *Baltimore Sun*, May 29, 2015 <http://www.baltimoresun.com/news/maryland/bs-md-omalley-zero-tolerance-20150529-story.html>.

259. Natsai Todd, "#Callmeout: dream hampton gets dragged," *The Femini*, August 19, 2015 <http://thefemini.com/2015/08/19/callemout-dream-hampton-gets-dragged/>. This blog post includes leaked screenshots of an IM exchange between the hip-hop writer dream hampton (lowercase in original) and BLM activist Erika Totten revealing that Sanders' invitations were rebuffed, and showing intense infighting among the would-be leaders of this allegedly leaderless movement.

260. <https://twitter.com/WyzeChef/status/633333599043883008>.

261. <https://twitter.com/deray/status/648590191746285570>;
     <https://twitter.com/deray/status/650504622499594240>.

262. "Full transcript: Hillary Clinton convo with #BlackLives
     Matter," *Politics365*, August 18, 2015 <http://politic365.
     com/2015/08/18/full-transcript-hillary-clinton-convo-with-
     blacklivesmatter/>.

263. <http://blacklivesmatter.com/guiding-principles/>.

264. <https://www.facebook.com/BlackLivesMatter/
     posts/488330528004864>

265. Touré F. Reed, "Why liberals separate race from class," *Jacobin*,
     August 22, 2015 <https://www.jacobinmag.com/2015/08/bernie-
     sanders-black-lives-matter-civil-rights-movement/>.

266. Leah N. Gordon, *From Power to Prejudice: The Rise of Racial
     Individualism in Midcentury America* (Chicago: University of
     Chicago Press, 2015).

267. <http://www.washingtonpost.com/graphics/national/police-
     shootings/>.

268. Jamiles Lartey, "By the numbers: US police killed more in days
     than other countries do in years," *The Guardian*, June 9, 2015
     <http://www.theguardian.com/us-news/2015/jun/09/the-
     counted-police-killings-us-vs-other-countries>.

269. The Sentencing Project, *Fact Sheet: Trends in U.S. Corrections*, n.d.
     <http://sentencingproject.org/doc/publications/inc_Trends_in_
     Corrections_Fact_sheet.pdf>.

270. Seth Ackerman, "Truly too hot for Jacobin," *Too Hot for Jacobin*,
     February 5, 2015 <http://toohotforjacobin.blogspot.com/2015/02/
     truly-too-hot-for-jacobin.html>.

271. Jim Galloway, "John Lewis on Bernie Sanders: 'There's not anything free in America,'" *Atlanta Journal-Constitution* Political Insider blog, February 17, 2016 <http://politics.blog.myajc.com/2016/02/17/john-lewis-on-bernie-sanders-nothing-free-in-america/>.

272. H. Bruce Franklin, "The American prison in the culture wars," *Workplace: A Journal for Academic Labor*, December 2000 <http://louisville.edu/journal/workplace/issue6/franklin.html>.

273. Paul Krugman, "My unicorn problem," *New York Times*, February 16, 2016 <http://krugman.blogs.nytimes.com/2016/02/16/my-unicorn-problem/>.

274. Ezra Klein, "Bernie Sanders's single-payer plan isn't a plan at all," *Vox*, January 17, 2016 <http://www.vox.com/2016/1/17/10784528/bernie-sanders-single-payer-health-care>.

275. Seth Ackerman, "Meet the new Harry and Louise," *Jacobin*, January 25, 2016 <https://www.jacobinmag.com/2016/01/vox-bernie-sanders-single-payer-ezra-klein-matt-yglesias/>.

276. Jackie Calmes, "Left-leaning economists question cost of Bernie Sanders's plans," *New York Times*, February 15, 2016 <http://www.nytimes.com/2016/02/16/us/politics/left-leaning-economists-question-cost-of-bernie-sanderss-plans.html>.

277. Pepe Escobar, "We are a banana republic," *Asia Times*, May 19, 2005 <http://www.atimes.com/atimes/Global_Economy/GE19Dj01.html>.

278. Paul Starr, "Why Democrats should beware Sanders' socialism," *Politico Magazine*, February 22, 2016 <http://www.

politico.com/magazine/story/2016/02/bernie-sanders-2016-socialism-213667>.

279. Doug Henwood, "I'm borrowing my way through college," *Left Business Observer* No. 125, February 2010 <http://leftbusinessobserver.com/College.html>.

280. Single-payer is just one way of organizing a public health insurance system. Under such a model, providers remain private and the government pays the bills. That is, only the insurance function is socialized. This is how it works in Canada. Under Britain's National Health Service, everything is socialized: doctors are public employees and hospitals are government-owned. Sanders is proposing the former, even though the British system is far cheaper to run than the Canadian.

281. Andrew Dugan, "Cost still delays healthcare for about one in three in U.S.," Gallup, November 30, 2015 <http://www.gallup.com/poll/187190/cost-delays-healthcare-one-three.aspx>; Physicians for a National Health Program, "What is a health savings account?," n.d. <http://www.pnhp.org/facts/hsa.pdf>.

282. OECD health data from <http://www.oecd.org/els/health-systems/health-data.htm>.

283. <http://www.census.gov/newsroom/press-releases/2015/cb15-157.html>, <http://www.gallup.com/poll/188045/uninsured-rate-fourth-quarter-2015.aspx>.

284. Amy Chozick and Patrick Healy, "Inside the Clinton Team's Plan to Defeat Donald Trump," *New York Times*, February 29, 2016 <http://www.nytimes.com/2016/03/01/us/politics/hillary-clinton-donald-trump-general-election.html?_r=0>.

285. Edward Luce, "Trump has the White House in his sights," *Financial Times*, February 28, 2016 <http://www.ft.com/intl/cms/s/0/0c983610-dc83-11e5-8541-00fb33bdf038.html#axzz42lBlvhk8>.

286. Ryan Lizza, "The great divide," *New Yorker*, March 21, 2016 <http://www.newyorker.com/magazine/2016/03/21/bernie-hillary-and-the-new-democratic-party>.

287. Kate Andersen Brower, *The Residence: Inside the Private World of the White House* (New York: HarperCollins, 2015), p. 145.

288. Hillary D. Rodham's 1969 Student Commencement Speech <http://www.wellesley.edu/events/commencement/archives/1969commencement/studentspeech>.

289. Interview with NPR's *Weekend Edition*, January 13, 1996. Audio at <https://www.youtube.com/watch?v=h15-tiVWk-0>.

290. Morris, *Rewriting History*, p. 148.

291. Adam Nagourney, "Mrs. Clinton vows fight on issues and image," *New York Times*, February 6, 2000 <http://www.nytimes.com/2000/02/06/nyregion/mrs-clinton-vows-fight-on-issues-and-image.html>.

292. Jon Greenberg, "Hillary Clinton says she and Bill were 'dead broke,'" *PolitiFact*, June 10, 2014 <http://www.politifact.com/truth-o-meter/statements/2014/jun/10/hillary-clinton/hillary-clinton-says-she-and-bill-were-dead-broke/>.

293. Brian Ross, Maddy Sauer, and Rhonda Schwartz, "Clinton remained silent as Wal-Mart fought unions," ABC News, January 31, 2008 <http://abcnews.go.com/Blotter/story?id=4218509>. Video at <https://www.youtube.com/

watch?v=SnMZRvzcQww>.

294. Gwen Ifill, "The 1992 campaign: Hillary Clinton defends her conduct in law firm," *New York Times*, March 17, 1992 <http://www.nytimes.com/1992/03/17/us/the-1992-campaign-hillary-clinton-defends-her-conduct-in-law-firm.html>; Bernstein, *A Woman in Charge*, Kindle loc. 1668–1669.

295. Christopher Massie, "Hillary Clinton used to talk about how the people on welfare were 'no longer deadbeats,'" *BuzzFeed*, July 21, 2015 <http://www.buzzfeed.com/christophermassie/hillary-clinton-used-to-talk-about-how-the-people-on-welfare#.kl7VboAdpw>.

296. Clinton, *Living History*, pp. 369–370.

297. Ronald Kessler, *The First Family Detail: Secret Service Agents Reveal the Hidden Lives of the Presidents* (New York: Crown, 2014), p. 24.

298. "The CNN Democratic debate, annotated," *Washington Post*, October 13, 2015 <https://www.washingtonpost.com/news/the-fix/wp/2015/10/13/the-oct-13-democratic-debate-who-said-what-and-what-it-means/>.

299. <http://www.sentencingproject.org/doc/File/three%20strikes%20law_presidential.pdf>.

300. Hillary Clinton, "Remarks by the First Lady to the Ninth Annual 'Women in Policing' Awards, New York, New York," August 10, 1994 <http://clinton4.nara.gov/media/text/1994-08-10-first-lady-remarks-to-the-ninth-annual-women-in-policing-awards.text>.

301. Ben Smith, "Clinton tacks right at left-leaning forums," *Politico*, December 2, 2007 <http://www.politico.com/news/

stories/1207/7127.html>.

302. Brower, *The Residence*, p. 153; Kessler, *The First Family Detail*, p. 24.

303. Kessler, *First Family Detail*, p. 16.

304. Congressional Record, 107th Congress, October 10, 2002, p. S10288 <http://thomas.loc.gov/cgi-bin/query/F?r107:1:./temp/~r107couOQx:e520451:>.

305. David Sirota and Andrew Perez, "Campaign 2016: Hillary Clinton pitched Iraq as 'a business opportunity' for US corporations," *International Business Times*, September 30, 2015 <http://www.ibtimes.com/campaign-2016-hillary-clinton-pitched-iraq-business-opportunity-us-corporations-2121999>. The original email with the quote is at <https://www.scribd.com/doc/283273910/Clinton-Iraq-Email>.

306. Alex Dominguez, "Romney says Sen. Clinton 'timid' on Iran," *Washington Post*, February 2, 2007 <http://www.washingtonpost.com/wp-dyn/content/article/2007/02/02/AR2007020200430.html>.

307. David Morgan, "Clinton says U.S. could 'totally obliterate' Iran," Reuters, April 22, 2008 <http://www.reuters.com/article/2008/04/22/us-usa-politics-iran-idUSN2224332720080422>.

308. Angie Drobnic Holan, "Video shows tarmac welcome, no sniper fire," *PolitiFact*, March 25, 2008 <http://www.politifact.com/truth-o-meter/statements/2008/mar/25/hillary-clinton/video-shows-tarmac-welcome-no-snipers/>.

309. Corbett Daly, "Clinton on Qaddafi: "We came, we saw, he died," CBS News, October 20, 2011 <http://www.cbsnews.com/news/

clinton-on-qaddafi-we-came-we-saw-he-died/>.

310. Jeffrey Goldberg, "Hillary Clinton: 'Failure' to help Syrian rebels led to the rise of ISIS," *The Atlantic*, August 10, 2014 <http://www.theatlantic.com/international/archive/2014/08/hillary-clinton-failure-to-help-syrian-rebels-led-to-the-rise-of-isis/375832/>.

311. First seven quotes in this section from Domenico Montanaro, "A timeline of Hillary Clinton's evolution on trade," NPR, April 21, 2015 <http://www.npr.org/sections/itsallpoliti cs/2015/04/21/401123124/a-timeline-of-hillary-clintons-evolution-on-trade>.

312. Hillary Rodham Clinton, "Statement of Senator Clinton for the Congressional Record on Central American–Dominican Republic Free Trade Agreement," June 30, 2005 <http://web.archive.org/web/20050724051828/http://clinton.senate.gov/news/statements/details.cfm?id=240183&&>.

313. Emma Roller, "Hillary Clinton: Edward Snowden's leaks helped terrorists," *National Journal*, April 25, 2014 <http://www.nationaljournal.com/defense/2014/04/25/hillary-clinton-edward-snowdens-leaks-helped-terrorists>.

314. Zeke J. Miller, "Clinton jokes about email investigation," *Time*, August 14, 2015 <http://time.com/3999368/hillary-clinton-emails-investigation-joke/>.

315. Annie Karni, "Allies fault Hillary Clinton's response on emails," *Politico*, August 19, 2015 <http://www.politico.com/story/2015/08/allies-fault-hillary-clinton-response-on-emails-121509.html>.

316. The three quotes on abortion come from Tom Kuiper, *I've Always*

Been a Yankees Fan: Hillary Clinton in her Own Words (Los Angeles: World Ahead Publishing, 2006), Kindle loc. 641–648. This is a right-wing book with some dubious stuff in it, but I do want to acknowledge its usefulness in finding juicy quotes. These check out.

317. All four quotes from Amy Sherman, "Hillary Clinton's changing position on same-sex marriage," *PolitiFact*, June 17, 2015 <http://www.politifact.com/truth-o-meter/statements/2015/jun/17/hillary-clinton/hillary-clinton-change-position-same-sex-marriage/>.

318. Transcribed from video of Mitchell interview <http://www.msnbc.com/msnbc-news/watch/clinton-and-reagan-she-had-a-lot-of-courage-and-grit-642358339895>. Polly Mosendz, "Former First Lady Nancy Reagan watched thousands of LGBTQ people die of AIDS," *Teen Vogue*, March 9, 2016 <http://www.teenvogue.com/story/nancy-reagan-death-hiv-aids-legacy>. Mark Joseph Stern, "Listen to Reagan's press secretary laugh about gay people dying of AIDS," *Slate*, December 1, 2015 <http://www.slate.com/blogs/outward/2015/12/01/reagan_press_secretary_laughs_about_gay_people_dying_of_aids.html>. Chris Geidner, "Nancy Reagan turned down Rock Hudson's plea for help nine weeks before he died," *BuzzFeed*, February 2, 2015 <http://www.buzzfeed.com/chrisgeidner/nancy-reagan-turned-down-rock-hudsons-plea-for-help-seven-we#.scwzqBDG3e>.

319. Tweet by *New York Times* reporter Amy Chozick: <https://twitter.com/amychozick/status/708713916415741953>.

320. Photo and thank-you note: <https://twitter.com/ariannaijones/status/708718147357057024>. Video of press conference: <http://www.c-span.org/video/?c4536221/hillary-clinton-bernie-

sanders-1993>.

321. Post Editorial Board, "Hillary Clinton's flip-flop on immigration," *New York Post*, July 8, 2015 <http://nypost.com/2015/07/08/ hillary-clintons-flip-flop-on-immigration/>; Chris Stirewalt, "Uncovered audio: Hillary was 'adamantly against illegal immigrants," *Fox News*, May 7, 2015 <http://www.foxnews.com/ politics/2015/05/07/uncovered-audio-hillary-was-adamantly- against-illegal-immigrants/>. Audio at <https://www.youtube. com/watch?v=VxASD4jHgCk>. Jose A. DelReal, "This time, Hillary Clinton supports giving driver's licenses to undocumented immigrants," *Washington Post*, April 16, 2015 <http://www. washingtonpost.com/news/post-politics/wp/2015/04/16/ this-time-hillary-clinton-supports-giving-drivers-licenses-to- undocumented-immigrants/>.

322. Transcript, CNN Town Hall, June 17, 2014 <http://transcripts.cnn. com/TRANSCRIPTS/1406/17/se.01.html>; Roque Planas, "Hillary Clinton defends call to deport child migrants," *Huffington Post*, August 19, 2015 < http://www.huffingtonpost.com/entry/hillary- clinton-child-migrants_55d4a5c5e4b055a6dab24c2f>.

323. Jarrett Murphy, "Hillary regrets Gandhi joke," CBS News, January 7, 2004 <http://www.cbsnews.com/news/hillary- regrets-gandhi-joke/>. Video at <https://www.youtube.com/ watch?v=e1Mq8kOXV_E>.

324. Kathy Kiely and Jill Lawrence, "Clinton makes case for wide appeal," *USA Today*, May 8, 2008 <http://usatoday30.usatoday. com/news/politics/election2008/2008-05-07-clintoninterview_N. htm>.

325. *Los Angeles Times*, September 8, 1998.

326. "Hillary's first joint interview—next to Bill in '92," CBS News, February 1, 2013 <http://www.cbsnews.com/news/hillarys-first-joint-interview-next-to-bill-in-92/>.

327. Sheehy, *Hillary's Choice*, Kindle loc. 3067–3068.

328. Interview with *Talk* magazine, quoted in Duncan Campbell, "Hillary explains away Clinton's infidelity," *The Guardian*, August 1, 1999 <http://www.theguardian.com/world/1999/aug/02/clinton.usa>.

329. Josh Vorhees, "A transcript of all Hillary Clinton's non-answers in her first cable TV interview of the race," *Slate*, July 7, 2015 <http://www.slate.com/blogs/the_slatest/2015/07/07/hillary_clinton_cnn_interview_a_heavily_edited_transcript_of_the_first_national.html>.

330. Doug Henwood, "Stop Hillary!," *Harper's*, November 2014 <http://harpers.org/archive/2014/10/stop-hillary-2/>.

331. Michelle Goldberg, "How David Brock built an empire to put Hillary in the White House," *The Nation*, December 15–22, 2014 <http://www.thenation.com/article/how-david-brock-built-empire-put-hillary-white-house/>.

332. Joe Conason, "Stop Hillary? Not with these mistakes (or the wisdom of Dick Morris)," *The National Memo*, October 27, 2014 <http://www.nationalmemo.com/stop-hillary-mistakes-wisdom-dick-morris/>.

INDEX